DAVID DULMAGE
7808 VERNON RDS.
CLAY, NY 13041

W9-BIW-277

*The Spirit-filled church
is not a gathering of spectators,
but a company of eager participants,
each of whom carries the
responsibility of participating
in and contributing to the act
of corporate worship in a
distinctly personal way.*
—John Lancaster

The Spirit-filled Church

JOHN LANCASTER

GOSPEL PUBLISHING HOUSE
SPRINGFIELD, MISSOURI
02-0601

THE SPIRIT-FILLED CHURCH
Published 1973 by the
Elim Pentecostal Churches
Great Britain

American Edition © 1975
By the Gospel Publishing House
Springfield, Missouri 65802
Printed in the United States of America

ISBN 0-88243-601-5

To
Dorothy
My Companion On
The Emmaus Road

Introduction

Some time ago I came across an article by Dr. Martyn Lloyd-Jones on the subject of revival which challenged me. He was answering the objection that "nowhere in the New Testament are we taught to pray for revival," and he pointed out that this was because the writers of the New Testament were living in an atmosphere of revival. He added: "What we read about the Church in the New Testament is an account of revival. The New Testament Church was full of the power of the Spirit. The Church of the New Testament was a pneumatic church, filled with the Spirit." (*How Shall They Hear?* p. 49.)

Then I came across some words written by another author in a completely different context. They were written by the Dutch theologian, W. C. van Unnik, in *New Testament Studies*, a symposium which was published in memory of T. W. Manson, in which van Unnik discussed the nature of the Spirit's activities in the life and worship of the Early Church. Commenting on 1 Corinthians 14:25, he remarked: "This picture of a service in the apostolic age shows that these Christians came together in a pneumatic atmosphere, filled by the Pneuma of God." A little later on in the same chapter he wrote that Christian worship stood in what he called "this magnetic field of the Holy Spirit."

I was struck by the way in which two very different

writers were conscious of what they both called the "pneumatic," or Spirit-filled, atmosphere of the New Testament Church. I was reminded of J. B. Phillips's remark that, when he was translating the New Testament, he felt like an electrician working in an old house in which a lot of the wires were still live. Obviously, then, the first Church was unmistakably Spirit-filled and, even at the distance of 2,000 years, its live, Spirit-charged atmosphere comes across. If this was so of the Early Church, ought it not to be so of the Church today?

We have much cause to thank God that, since the beginning of this century, first in the worldwide Pentecostal Movement and now increasingly in the historic denominations, there has come a return to that Spirit-filled condition. "All over the world, the Spirit is moving," and for this we lift our hearts in grateful praise.

At the same time, there is an ever-increasing need for us to understand the basic principles of a Spirit-filled Church, and especially insofar as they touch upon our responsibilities as individual members. If we believe that the "magnetic field" of the Spirit's active presence is the proper location of the Church at all times, then it is important that we should know how to stay in that location. If we believe that the New Testament experience of Pentecostal power and blessing is the norm for the Church today, then we must try to understand how that experience was entered into and maintained.

The purpose of this book, then, is to look at the teaching of the New Testament and attempt to relate it to our own situation. It has been written with my own Fellowship—the Elim Pentecostal Church—in mind, though I hope it will be of help to many others. I have tried to take an overall view of the Spirit-filled

Church rather than concentrating in detail on particular aspects. For this reason, there is no specific chapter on the gifts of the Spirit, since I have tried to see them not in isolation but as parts of a more general way of spiritual life. Above all, I have endeavored to be as practical as possible. My book pretends to no new insights; rather it is a restatement of things most surely believed in the hope that it will stir up the minds of many by way of remembrance and be a steadying hand to those second- and third-generation Pentecostals growing up in our midst, who, I trust, will climb higher than their fathers.

In his book *Thine Is the Kingdom*, James S. Stewart wrote the following stirring passage: "It is a verifiable phenomenon of Christian experience that an individual man, laid hold upon by the Spiril of God, can have his whole being lifted to a level of spiritual force and efficacy which previously would have seemed quite incredible; and if the Spirit of God can do such mighty works for and in and by one life surrendered to His sway, what a revolutionizing of history might not result from a fully committed Church?"

It is my prayer that this volume may help to bring some of us nearer to that ideal.

Contents

1

Its Doctrine

One of the truly remarkable things about the first Pentecostal Church was the way in which it was so rapidly molded into a well-ordered community. When one considers the extraordinary events which accompanied its birth—the supernatural phenomena of wind and fire and speaking in tongues, the overwhelming response to the preaching, and the infectious joy which permeated its fellowship—one cannot but be impressed by the absence of fanaticism and the orderliness with which its fellowship was maintained. The mighty, rushing wind of the Spirit might blow disturbingly through the corridors of ecclesiastical power, demolishing some of the ornate structures of formal religion which lay across its path, but within the fellowship of those who received the power of the Spirit, no place was given to excess. The Spirit-filled leaders of the Early Church never allowed it to degenerate into a motley rabble of enthusiasts.

It is highly significant, therefore, that when Luke begins to describe the life of the Early Church, he begins with a reference to its doctrine. From the very beginning, the leaders of the Church insisted that its members should be well instructed in the essentials of the faith. In order to achieve this, they established regular teaching sessions to which the converts were expected to come. That this was not a casual, optional thing is indicated by the words Luke employs in Acts 2:42: "They continued steadfastly," or, as the RSV renders it, "They devoted themselves to the apostles' teaching." The verb employed here embodies the idea of perseverance, and is used in Acts 1:14 of the concentrated praying of the disciples, and again in Acts 6:4 of the apostles' determination to give themselves to the study of the Word. It is worthy of note that, while doubtless it was the apostles who initiated these teaching sessions, the converts themselves were no less ready to learn and "devoted themselves" to the apostles' teaching. This emphasis on doctrine was one of the stabilizing factors which steadied the infant Church in those exciting days.

Because of its very nature, a Spirit-filled church stands in special need of sound doctrine. Generally speaking, the average Pentecostal church has a comparatively loose structure. Though it may have a full-time minister and, in some cases, regrettably, leaves too much to him, on the whole the division between the minister and the people is far less distinct than in more formal churches. The open type of worship provides for a far broader participation by all the members, and there are no liturgical railroad tracks to make sure that nothing unexpected happens. In addition, and perhaps most important, the spontaneous nature of the exercise of spiritual gifts such as prophecy and interpretation of tongues creates a situation in which sound doctrine is essential both as the guardian of truth and the guarantee of good order.

Throughout the history of the Church, the tension between the freedom of the Spirit and the need for order has created one of the greatest spiritual problems. Paul saw this when he wrote to the Galatians urging them to stand fast in their newfound freedom

14

in Christ (Galatians 5:1), at the same time warning them against the danger of allowing that freedom to lead to disorder (Galatians 5:13). On the other hand, he found it necessary, while congratulating the Colossians on their good order (Colossians 2:5, RSV), to warn them against the ever-present danger of creating a legalistic system (vv. 20-23). Liberty always tends towards license; law always tends towards legalism. It is very difficult, it seems, even for Christians to avoid the swing of the pendulum from one extreme to another.

Nowhere is the need for true balance more acute than in a Pentecostal church. We rightly believe in the spontaneity of the Spirit, who moves in sovereign freedom, invisible yet dynamic, even as the "wind bloweth where it listeth." Believing this, we rightly reject the deadening hand of religious tradition which so often would restrain that freedom. In the rigid structures and cold formalities of much organized religion, the Spirit has been grieved and quenched. Like men whose lungs are bursting for a breath of God's pure air, we can no longer stand the stuffy atmosphere, but feel like breaking all the windows and dispensing with all structures in order to enjoy the freedom of the Spirit. The danger is, however, that, in our attempt to break out into freedom, we expose ourselves to the very things from which we desire to escape.

A classic example of this is found in the Montanist movement which flourished in the second half of the second century after Christ. Its leader, Montanus, preached a message which in many respects had the characteristics of many revival movements: a strong emphasis on the manifestation of the Spirit; a demand for personal holiness; and an eager anticipation of the Lord's second coming. In many ways, the movement was a protest against the growing worldliness of professing Christianily. The tragedy of Montanism lay in the fact that, in its reaction against the prevailing situation in the Church, it went to the opposite extreme. Its emphasis on the charismatic became so great that in the end, the utterances of its prophets, and especially of its prophetesses, carried more weight than the Scriptures themselves. Thus the door to dangerous error was opened. Likewise its demand for holiness became oppressive and created a bondage as rigid as the very system from which it had sought freedom.

The dangers of Montanism are always present wherever the so-called freedom of the Spirit is set over against the authority of the Word of God. God cannot deny himself (2 Timothy 2:13), nor can He contradict himself. It is therefore inconceivable that manifestations or utterances inspired by the Holy Spirit should in any way conflict with the plain teaching of the Word of God. The final authority of the Scriptures must be made the standard by which all utterances and practices are judged. Paul's words to the Corinthians (1 Corinthians 14:29) make it clear that prophetic utterances are not to be accepted at face value, but are to be subjected to the careful judgment of spiritual men. The final court of appeal in such judgment plainly must be the Word of God.

The fate of Montanus and his enthusiastic, but ultimately misguided, followers is a warning to every charismatic movement. Jumping the rails of formal religion is no excuse for a kind of Pentecostal "freeway madness." Freedom is exhilarating, but it can be disastrous. Unless our experience of the supernatural is governed by the principles contained in the Scriptures, we run the grave danger of self-destruction. One of the disturbing things about the neo-Pentecostal Movement is its apparent willingness to set greater value on Spirit-baptism than on Biblical truth as the basis for true fellowship, so that, under its broad umbrella, men who deny the authority of Scripture and some of the basic doctrines of the Christian faith may link arms with conservative evangelicals on the one hand and convinced Romanists on the other. The test of acceptance, it seems, has become charismatic experience rather than scriptural faith. Is this really the unity of the Spirit, or is it a kind of modern Montanism in which the ecstatic experience has replaced the authority of the Word? If it is the latter, it is already sowing the seeds of its own destruction. Let those of us in the so-called "classical" Pentecostal churches, whose comparatively longer experience of these things has given us certain advantages, take heed lest we likewise fall.

What, then, was the apostles' doctrine? It is not the purpose of this chapter to embark on a detailed examination of this, but rather to suggest some of the basic truths which are essential to a truly Spirit-filled church. It is doubtful whether, at this early stage of the Church's existence, there had been time to systematize fully the truths for which Christianity was to become distinctive. It was only later, in the great Epistles of the New Testament, that the apostles' doctrine received fuller exposition. Nevertheless, it was still possible, even in those early days, to instruct the converts in the foundation truths of the Faith.

It is clear from the closing chapter of the Gospel of Luke and the opening verses of the Book of Acts that the apostles regarded the authority of Scripture as final. They may not have had a formal statement on the Doctrine of Inspiration, but they clearly recognized where the source of authority lay. Both on the road to Emmaus (Luke 24:27) and later in the Upper Room (v. 45), the Lord Jesus "opened the scriptures"

17

to His disciples. He not only interpreted to them the significance of His own person and work, but He also impressed upon them the vital importance of Scripture as the basis of belief. It can hardly be doubted that in the remaining 40 days of His fellowship with them, during which time He taught them regarding the Kingdom of God (Acts 1:3), He made constant appeal to the Old Testament as the basis for His teaching. It is therefore not surprising that, as recorded throughout the Book of Acts, the apostles looked to the Scriptures for their final authority. Whether it be in the matter of choosing a successor for the ill-fated Judas (Acts 1:16), or explaining the phenomena of the Day of Pentecost (Acts 2:16f), or crying out to God for spiritual enabling (Acts 4:24-26), or discussing the problems raised by the admission of Gentiles to the Church (Acts 15:5), it was to Scripture that they constantly turned. Their preaching, praying, and decision-making were governed by what the Scriptures taught.

Let there be no mistake. The first Pentecostal Church stood foursquare on the Word of God. Whatever abundance of spiritual gifts it enjoyed, however exhilarating the supernatural experiences it constantly encountered, the Early Church never lost sight of the fact that the Word of God, revealed originally in the Old Testament and subsequently in the New, provided both the foundation of true doctrine and the basis of an ongoing spiritual life. Thus Paul, saying farewell to the leaders of the Ephesian Church and conscious of the perils which would assail that church in days to come, said, "And now, brethren, I commend you to God, and to the word of his grace, which is able to build you up" (Acts 20:32).

A Spirit-filled church which either rejects or ignores the Spirit-inspired Word is a contradiction in terms.

No one can read the Book of Acts without being deeply impressed by the tremendous emphasis on the person and work of Christ in the preaching of the apostles. "They ceased not to teach and preach Jesus Christ" (Acts 5:42). Not only was the death and resurrection of Christ the basis of the gospel they proclaimed to a sinful world, but the lordship of Christ was the foundation of their corporate life as the Church and the point of reference for every aspect of their personal life as individual believers.

This Christ-centeredness comes out even more clearly in the Epistles, in which the "apostles' doctrine" received its more detailed exposition. The believer is shown to be a man "in Christ," that is, a man whose salvation from sin depends on Christ, whose personal spiritual life can be maintained only by an ongoing relationship with Christ, and whose place in the Church can be realized only through personal submission to the lordship of Christ. Indeed, the final hope of the Christian, gleaming like sunrise on the distant hills, is inextricably bound up with what Christ is and does—it is "Christ in you, the hope of glory" (Colossians 1:27).

This emphasis on the Lord Jesus Christ must never be forgotten. As Pentecostals we are more than "The Tongues People." It is true that we have certain points of emphasis in our doctrinal position, but our message must be seen in its total perspective. Our special insights must never loom so large that they obscure the full truth as it is in Christ, otherwise the so-called "full gospel" becomes an enlarged detail and we lose the vast sweep, the depth, and color of the divine masterpiece.

2
It's Future

We may sometimes feel that the much-used formula "the foursquare gospel" is inadequate to express the full truth to which the Spirit-filled church is committed. Certainly it is a restricted—and sometimes restricting—statement of belief, yet it shows something of the wisdom of the early Pentecostals in that it firmly rooted their distinctive doctrines in the person of Christ. It emphasized their conviction that in Jesus Christ salvation, healing, the baptism in the Holy Spirit, and the final hope of the Second Coming were centered. Provided that we are prepared to move beyond some of the well-worn clichés and think seriously about the implications of the foursquare gospel, we shall find that it is not superficial at all.

It is the declaration of an eschatological purpose. It declares that Jesus is the Coming King. This aspect of truth comes last in the statement, but only because the formula of the foursquare gospel puts things in their chronological order and therefore sees the Second Coming as the climax of God's purpose in Christ. Logically, however, the doctrine of the last things must come first. This is the "one far-off divine event to which the whole creation moves," and it is therefore the ultimate message of the gospel, from which the acts of God in history and through the Church find their real meaning.

What do we mean by eschatology? What do we have in mind when we preach Christ as "Coming King"? There is a danger that we are overly concerned with the enigmatic (the interpretation of the fascinating symbolism of the prophetic Scriptures) or with the dramatic (imaginative descriptions of apocalyptic disasters, and intriguing speculations about the space travels of the saints and the material splendors of the golden age). We must never lose sight of the real emphasis of true eschatology, for the Bible is not so much concerned with satisfying our curiosity about the exact details of the future as with reminding us of the overall purpose of God and the relation of history and personal experience to that purpose.

Biblically, the doctrine of the last things is a statement of the sovereignty of God. He "upholds all things by the word of his power" (Hebrews 1:3), by Him all things "hold together" as a coherent whole (Colossians 1:17), and thus the final destiny of the universe is completely in His jurisdiction. He has "subjected it in hope" (Romans 8:19-22) and therefore its sufferings are not death throes but birth pangs. He has put it in His storehouse, reserving it for apocalyptic fires which will not merely destroy its worthless elements but be the prelude to a new creation (2 Peter 3:7-13). He will discard it as a man throws off an outworn garment, replacing a threadbare cosmos with a new creation, and clothing himself in the garments of perpetual praise (Hebrews 1:10-12). Thus, while we must not ignore the warnings of the nuclear physicist about the threat of radioactive extinction, or those of the ecologist about the dangers of pollution, neither must we ever forget that in the last analysis the destiny of the world does not lie in the hands of some trigger-happy politician in the Kremlin or in Washington, but in the control of a God of infinite wisdom and power. We must never become complacent about the problems posed by the diminishing resources of the earth and its growing pollution—indeed, as Christians, we ought to be far more concerned than we are—yet we must not regard these things in themselves as the final key to man's existence in the future.

The message of the Second Coming not only affirms God's sovereignty over the very physical structure of the universe; it also declares His control of history. Psalm 2 depicts a world seething with revolt, multitudes, led by their political leaders, in a mass demonstration against the sovereignty of God, but the puny protests are engulfed in the thunderous proclamation of God: "Yet have I set my king upon my holy hill of Zion." In the end there is no argument for, as Nebuchadnezzar was made to realize, "He doeth according to his will in the army of heaven, and among the inhabitants of the earth: and none can stay his hand, or say unto him, What doest thou?" (Daniel 4:35). The united testimony of the Old Testament and the New is to the fact that God not only sustains life through His providential care, but that He reigns. It was this hope that nerved the Jewish nation through its long years of pilgrimmage, conflict, and captivity—and still inspires the remnant—and it is this hope which has burned brightly as a beacon in the darkness to give the Church her final confidence. However dark the hour has been, however oppressive have been the forces of evil, however much righteous blood has been shed, however fragile the Church has appeared, however perplexing the distressing dilemmas of life have become, however inadequate men of God have been to interpret the mysteries attached to God's revelation of himself and His purpose, there is one cry that breaks out in the Apocalypse and gathers into itself all the confidence of the centuries: it is the great, heartlifting shout that surges from every corner of heaven, "Alleluia: for the Lord God omnipotent reigneth" (Revelation 19:6).

This is not an abstract hope, a wistful daydream of some distant golden age. Its concrete realities are being worked out in the affairs of men and nations. It must never be forgotten that God initiates history. He is not left to afterthoughts; He is not merely a mender of broken earthenware, but the inspired originator of a grand design. He is not merely piecing together man's mistakes, He is the architect of destiny. Thus the truth of the Second Coming must be seen not merely as a divine rescue operation, but as the climax to which God has been guiding history from its commencement, a climax which will bring Christ to earth again, not only as Saviour, but as Judge. It is significant that, on two occasions where it gives details of sermons preached to Gentiles—in Cornelius's house (Acts 10:42) and on Mars Hill (Acts 17:22)—the Book of Acts includes this emphasis on coming judgment. Perhaps this is a timely reminder that the message which is preached to our present post-Christian, and therefore pagan, society must also contain this solemn note (though, let it be added, it must be preached with all the tender concern which made the Master foretell Jerusalem's doom with tears).

This great forward-looking emphasis embraces the whole purpose of God. It touches not only the physical structure of the universe and the long unfolding of human history, for it also involves the future of the Church and the life of individual Christians. For the Church it means the assurance of final triumph. He who said, "I will build my church, and the gates of hell shall not prevail against it," is coming again for her. In spite of her tragic failures and her sad divisions she is destined to become a royal Bride, a fitting consort for the King of kings (Ephesians 5:27; Revelation 21:2). We should be grieved over the many things in the Church which dishonor the name of Christ, and it is imperative that we should pray and strive continually for the renewal of the Church, but we must never lose sight of this divine determination to present the Church to her Lord and Master as a Bride adorned and without blemish. For the individual there is the challenging reminder of personal accountability. "We must all stand before the judgment seat of Christ" (2 Corinthians 5:10). We must all undergo the divine scrutiny (1 Corinthians 3:13-15) as to our stewardship. At the same time, however, there is the promise of personal transformation in which not only spiritually but also physically we are to be finally made into His likeness (Romans 8:29; 1 Corinthians 15:49; Philippians 3:21; 1 John 3:2).

The more we examine the life of the Early Church, the more we discover its emphasis on the second coming of Christ. Their prayers amid persecution were based on the conviction that God's sovereign control of history placed them in an invincible position (Acts 4:24-31). Their preaching emphasized not only that Jesus was Saviour, but that He was King and that He was coming again (Acts 17:7, 31; 1 Thessalonians 1:9, 10). Their motives were molded by a deep sense of responsibility, because they believed the second coming of Christ would bring them before His throne to give account (2 Corinthians 5:10, 11). Their central act of worship, the Lord's Supper, focused their thinking regularly on the fact that it was only "till He come" (1 Corinthians 11:26). As Canon Michael Green has observed: "The supreme spur to holy living and dedicated missionary work was this consciousness of the imminence of the end, of the limitations on the opportunities for evangelism, of the ultimate accountability

24

we all have to God." (*Evangelism in the Early Church*.)

Not less impressive is the way in which the New Testament places the Pentecostal aspect of the gospel in a strongly eschatological context. Thus Peter immediately refers to Joel's prophecy in explanation of the events of the Day of Pentecost and sets them in "the last days," reminding the multitudes that all that they saw and heard was part of the prelude to "that **great and notable day of the Lord**" (Acts 2:16-20). Similarly, when Paul refers to the work of the Spirit in the believer, however far we are prepared to go in our interpretation of his words, he sees it in its ultimate setting. In Romans 8:23 it is "first fruits," a term which indicates that the full harvest is yet to come. On three occasions (2 Corinthians 1:22; 5:5; Ephesians 1:13, 14) he uses the Greek word *arrabon*, rendered "earnest" in the AV and "guarantee" in the RSV. It speaks of a deposit or down payment which looks forward to future completion. W. E. Vine has pointed out that, in modern Greek, the word *arrabona* is the name given to an engagement ring. Our great Pentecostal heritage, then, is but the first installment of God's great provision. As yet we have only "tasted . . . the powers of the age to come" (Hebrews 6:5), and undreamed-of possibilities lie before us. Tongues and prophecy may eventually cease, but only because that which is perfect will then have come. They cease, not because they are inferior, but because they are adaptations, limited to our present circumstances, of the vast resources of the eternal realm. The true Pentecostalist, far from hugging the gifts of the Spirit to himself as God's final provision, sees them rather as a gracious promise of future glory and yearns to move out into that age where, free from earthly limitation, he can enjoy the "exceeding weight of glory."

25

3

Its Message

The Spirit-filled Church proclaims the message of a redemptive intervention. It declares that Jesus Christ is the Saviour and the Healer. Its eschatological hope is meaningless unless there is clear evidence that the power of sin and death has been broken. A church which is only concerned with dreams about the future and does not come to terms with the realities of the present deserves the old agnostic jibe that it is only concerned with pie in the sky. As a young man in the Royal Air Force, I was sometimes subjected to irreverent renderings of perverted versions of such songs as "There is a happy land, far, far away" or "Shall we gather at the river?" but though my colleagues did this as an intended sneer at Christian faith, I could not help recognizing that, to the unconverted man, much of the gospel seems irrelevant to the harsh facts of everyday life and will remain so unless it is fully and properly proclaimed.

The Spirit-filled church is not a club for researchers in the supernatural, or a fraternity for students of prophecy, but a base from which an urgent rescue operation must be maintained. We must never lose sight of the ultimate purpose of God in history, nor must we lose sight of the immediate needs of the men and women around us. We must come to terms with the uncomfortable truth of man's sin and his utter inability to realize his own yearning for self-conquest and unfettered happiness. We must force ourselves to look with compassionate eyes on the appalling casualties that litter our own Jericho road. We must believe with all our hearts that the gospel really is the power of God unto salvation. "There is none other name under heaven given among men, whereby we must be saved" (Acts 4:12).

The truly Pentecostal message is therefore consistent with Biblical doctrine. It declares the doctrine of man as it is revealed in Scripture—man made in the image of God, destined for dominion, but fallen through sin. It declares that sin is universal and that the wrath of God is revealed from heaven against all ungodliness and unrighteousness of men (Romans 1:18). Evil and suffering take many forms and there are therefore many secondary ways of ministering to human need, but the basic problem of the human heart remains the same. The only effective answer to that basic need is the gospel, the good news of what God has done through the death and resurrection of Christ. Never for one moment must we become insensitive to the tragic, heart-breaking needs of our world: its poverty, hunger, injustice, inequalities, despair, and cynicism. Too often we have snuggled cozily down into our evangelical blankets and shut our eyes against the obscene wickedness of human greed and its social consequences, or at best have signed a petition here, or sent a donation there, without ever really coming to terms with the real needs of people within personal reach. It is so much easier to look at statistics than to face people, so much easier to join a protest march than to get involved with the family next door. When we have said this, however, we must never forget that, in the end, the real need of the world is salvation from the power of sin. If we are not careful we can spend our time and energy dealing with symptoms rather than causes.

The Spirit-filled church must therefore remember that its first charge is to preach the gospel, to declare the facts of sin and judgment and to proclaim God's historic intervention in the person and work of Jesus Christ. The Atonement is central to the Pentecostal message, because it is central to all God's dealings with a fallen race. Jesus Christ is Saviour and Healer, because He has effectively dealt with sin and its consequences through His death and resurrection.

It must never be forgotten, however, that salvation is far more than merely extricating sinners from awkward situations. It is not merely a question of wiping out moral debts or even of granting pardon to guilty men, nor is it simply the release of reprieved offenders. It has in view the total renewal of the penitent man. God's purpose in Christ is to take men who have been disfigured by sin and remake them in the image of His Son (Romans 8:29). Forgiveness and release from the guilt and penalty of sin come into it, but the purpose of God is that every redeemed man should be fully restored to the "image of him that created him" (Colossians 3:10).

It is perhaps unfortunate that we have allowed too firm a distinction between the spiritual and physical aspects of man's being. We tend to think of men as souls to be saved, as though salvation extends only to the invisible, spiritual part of a man's being. The New Testament makes it clear that God has in view the total personality—what man is intellectually, emotionally, morally, spiritually, and physically. Sanctification embraces the whole man (Romans 12:1, 2; 1 Thessalonians 5:23), and the hope of immortality relates to the body of our humiliation as much as to our glorified spirits (Philippians 3:21). "Know ye not," says Paul to the Corinthians, that "your *bodies* are members of Christ?" and again, "Know ye not that your *body* is the temple of the Holy Ghost?" (1 Corinthians 6:19). Therefore, what we are physically is of deep concern to God, and this means not only that sanctification must be expressed through the physical details of my life, but also that God's saving act in Christ is concerned with my physical life as well as my spiritual experience (see also Romans 8:23).

This is not the place to discuss the full implications of divine healing. There are many problems to be honestly and humbly faced, but it cannot be denied that both in the ministry of the Lord Jesus (Acts 10:38) and in the outreach of the Early Church a compassionate, effective ministry to the sick was maintained. In many cases the miracles which occurred were granted in confirmation of the message preached, and especially in the Book of Acts there is strong evidence of a divine sovereignty in the ministry of healing, so that it was specific rather than general. We confidently assert, however, that healings and miracles were regarded in the New Testament as an important part of the evangelistic outreach. It is easy for us to rationalize our own failure by assuming that the comparative absence of such miracles today is because God has withdrawn His healing power or transferred it to the medical profession. We give thanks to God for the dedicated work of doctors and nurses, but we recognize that there are disturbing physical, mental, and nervous needs which challenge us, not only as human beings, but as the preachers of a gospel which touches the whole man. Have we become so influenced by the materialistic philosophies of our day that we no longer believe in the supernatural power of God? Have we assumed that God is really only interested in souls?

Does it seem to us less reasonable that He should rearrange blood cells or adjust the chemical or nervous structure of the body? Is it rather our loss of faith, the narrowness of our vision, or our uneasy avoidance of awkward problems that has led to the diminishing of the supernatural in our midst? Has God revised the terms of the original evangel, or is our failure apparent because somewhere we have retreated from the responsibility which the supernatural always brings? Perhaps these are the questions we need to ask—and answer honestly—before we jump to conclusions about divine healing.

4

Its Power

The Spirit-filled Church proclaims the message of a divine dynamic. For every generation there is a tension between the facts of the historic past and the promise of the prophetic future. The gospel declares that God has acted in Christ for man's salvation, and the prophetic Scriptures look hopefully to the day when God will fulfill His purpose for the universe. How does this affect us in the here and now? Facing the truth about ourselves, we are forced to cry with Tennyson:

> O for a man to arise in me
>
> That the man I am may cease to be.

Unless the answer is clearly declared, Christianity, for all its traditions and its splendid hopes, may seem irrelevant.

The Pentecostal message, however, declares that what God has already done in the past and what He proposes to do in the future are focused on the believer in his contemporary situation. He has "tasted the heavenly gift . . . become a partaker of the Holy Spirit . . . tasted the good word of God and the powers of the age to come" (Hebrews 6:4, 5). Jesus Christ, the Baptizer in the Holy Spirit, calls men not merely to acceptance of truth and to the joy of forgiveness, but also to the experience of a new divine dynamic.

The necessity of the ministry of the Spirit was clearly recognized in the Old Testament. The Law clearly defined the divine standards of conduct and inhibited the sinner by dire warnings of judgment, but it could not provide the necessary moral power by which its precepts might be kept (Romans 8:3). The prophets looked forward to the day when the Spirit of God would come to indwell the hearts of men and so provide the missing dynamic. Ezekiel (36:26, 27) and Joel (2:28) both foretold a new era when the will of God would be fulfilled, not by the oppressive restrictions of an outward set of regulations, but by the inward thrust of the Spirit of the Lord. The Spirit was not inactive even in those far-off days, for He brooded creatively amid the darkness at the dawn of history. He gave wisdom and strength to men chosen for special tasks, and He moved upon the prophets and inspired their speech, but the Old Testament looked forward to the day when those creative energies would be experienced, not by a small, spiritual elite, but by the people of God as a whole, from the humblest maidservant to the most gifted leader.

Today that dream has been realized. We live in the Age of the Spirit. Indeed, it is impossible even to be a Christian without having encountered the power of the Spirit. The Spirit convicts men of sin (John 16:8-11). Through the Spirit men are born again to new life in Christ (John 3:3-8). Without the Spirit it is impossible to acknowledge Christ as Lord in any genuine way (1 Corinthians 12:3). Whether we like it or not Christianity is inescapably supernatural. It is based upon a supernatural revelation through the Spirit-inspired Scripture and focused upon a supernatural Person, whose birth, life, death, and resurrection cannot be accounted for in merely human terms. Its power can be experienced only through the supernatural operation of the Holy Spirit at conversion, and its full dimensions can only be discovered through a continual response to the supernatural ministry of the Spirit and the Word.

The Spirit-filled Church believes that the dynamic of the Spirit is realized not only in regeneration and sanctification, but also in an enduement with power from on high, by which the believer is both renewed within himself and enabled to minister to the Church and to the world outside with an effectiveness which is not dependent on his own personal potential. "Ye shall receive power after that the Holy Ghost is come upon you" (Acts 1:8). It believes that this promise of power was given to men already regenerate with a view to equipping them for the specific tasks God has assigned to them. It concedes that the baptism in the Holy Spirit may coincide with conversion, but is convinced that it is not synonymous with conversion, since it is clear from the New Testament that the coming of the Spirit was recorded on several occasions as an event subsequent to conversion (Acts 2; 8:14; 9:17; and possibly 10:1).

The whole atmosphere of the Book of Acts and the references to the work of the Spirit in the Epistles suggest something rather more than the affably quiet notions we tend to have in our doctrine of the Spirit. He is symbolized by the mighty, rushing wind and the tongues of fire as well as by the gentle dove. The impact of His coming on those who received Him was outwardly discernible as well as inwardly potent. Simon "saw" that the Spirit was given (Acts 8:18). We are deeply grateful to God for the inward work of the Spirit, for

That gentle voice we hear,
Soft as the breath of even,
That checks each thought, and calms each fear
And speaks of heaven.

We dare not reduce God the Holy Ghost to a whisper, however. We must also sing

> There is no change in Thee,
> Lord God the Holy Ghost,
> Thy glorious majesty
> Is as at Pentecost!
> O may our loosened tongues proclaim
> That Thou, our God, art still the same.

I once heard Dr. Martyn Lloyd-Jones ask a meeting of ministers whether they or their congregations had ever experienced "joy unspeakable and full of glory" (1 Peter 1:8). "Don't water that down to mean just ordinary joy," he said. "Take it as it stands and ask yourself if you have ever really experienced anything that could honestly be described in those terms." He put his finger on one of our real problems. We have become so used to third-rate Christianity that we interpret the New Testament by our own standards. In so doing we empty it of its full meaning. We accuse the liberal theologian of emptying the Bible of its true meaning, but often we do the very same thing by our refusal to let it judge our contemporary life.

The Spirit-filled Church believes that the New Testament means what it says: that when it speaks of joy unspeakable and full of glory it means just this and not some watered-down substitute; that when it speaks of the *dunamis* of the Spirit it means real power and not simply a slight improvement. Above all, it believes that, when the New Testament says that Jesus Christ is the same yesterday and today and forever, it means what it says and that therefore we also may "touch Him in life's throng and press" and find wholeness and life. Because it believes that He is the same, it believes that the Church should be the same, that the pattern

34

set out in the Book of Acts is not a wistful vision of the good old days, but the norm for today.

This is no easy doctrine, but its challenge is exhilarating.

5

Its Membership

What constitutes a Spirit-filled church? The answer is Spirit-filled people. This looks like stating the obvious, but experience teaches us that it needs to be repeated again and again.

To begin with, we need to ask, "What is a church?" In the New Testament the word does not occur frequently, but whenever it does, it always refers to a body of people who have come together for a specific purpose. In Acts 19:39, for instance, the word *ekklesia*, the basic New Testament word for "church," is used in the speech of the town clerk of Ephesus when he is trying to cool down the angry mob that had gathered in the town's theater to demonstrate against the Christians. He urges them to disperse, telling them that if they had any genuine grounds for complaint they could be aired at the next "lawful assembly" (*ekklesia*), which was the name given to the regular meetings which met officially to discuss civic affairs. Even in a non-Christian context the word had a very definite meaning.

A church, then, is not simply a collection of people who happen to be together in the same place, but a community which has been called together and called out for a specific purpose. It does not consist of churchgoers or even of those who have undergone religious rites, but of those who have experienced the work of the Holy Spirit in their lives in converting and regenerating power.

The whole New Testament idea of the Church is not one of loose attachment, but of deep involvement. The Church is the body of Christ. This declares the inescapable involvement of every member in its corporate life (Ephesians 4:1-11). The Church is the bride of Christ. This requires wholehearted commitment to Him and intimate relationship with Him on the part of every member (Ephesians 5:23-33). The Church is the temple of the Holy Spirit. Every member is regarded as a living stone which must be integrated into the divinely designed structure (1 Peter 2:5-7).

Membership of the Church is not a matter of a casual acquaintance, but of definite commitment. It only really comes into being when a man or woman "gladly receives" the word of the gospel in such a way that they not only accept its truth intellectually, but submit to its authority over their own lives. The "word" which was received on the Day of Pentecost set forth Jesus Christ as Son of God and Saviour of men, a word which demanded repentance and baptism and which promised the remission of sins and the gift of the Spirit. To receive that word gladly meant submitting to its moral demands and thus experiencing its spiritual dynamic. The terms of membership are just the same today.

People who merely attend church on a Sunday may be on their way to becoming members of the Church. In many cases their very presence in the house of God indicates a work of grace within them and is the expression of a divinely aroused hunger for God. Unless church attendance eventually leads to commitment to Christ and to involvement in the life of the Church, however, it stops short of real Christian faith and experience. Sooner or later the all-important personal encounter with Jesus Christ must take place and His lordship must be acknowledged.

Some people cling to the church like a barnacle to the hull of a ship, but their names are not on the passenger list nor do they have any relationship with the Captain. They are attached, but they do not belong. Not until personal faith responds to the love of God in Christ do we really belong to the people of God.

Every man who becomes a Christian must be born again. He must consciously turn from his sin and receive Christ as Saviour and Lord. For this to happen he must have a personal encounter with the Holy Spirit.

The Spirit quickens men who are dead in trespasses and sins (2 Corinthians 3:6; Ephesians 2:1). The Spirit opens the eyes of men who have been blinded by the god of this world, and makes meaningful things which otherwise seem absurd (1 Corinthians 2:10-16). The Spirit convicts of sin (John 16:8-10) and brings release to men who have known nothing but bondage to the overbearing despotism of sin (Romans 8:2). The Spirit alone enables a man genuinely to acknowledge the lordship of Christ over his life (1 Corinthians 12:3). Our entrance into faith and thereby into the family of God is at every point dependent on the activity of the Spirit. Unless we are born of the Spirit we cannot enter the kingdom of God (John 3:5).

We must never forget, however, that the Spirit is not simply concerned with our initiation into the Christian faith; He is involved in every stage of our development as believers. Having begun in the Spirit, it is impossible for us to grow to maturity without Him (Galatians 3:3). In Romans 8 Paul makes it abundantly clear that true Christian experiences must be defined as life in the Spirit. The Spirit who has liberated us from the law of sin and death (v. 2), enables us to walk in newness of life (v. 4). Unless we have the Spirit within us, we do not belong to Christ (v. 9). Only if we set our minds on the things of the Spirit (v. 5) and are led by the Spirit (v. 14), can we know the enabling of the Spirit in our moral and spiritual conflict with the demands of the flesh (v. 13).

The Spirit "bears witness" to our true identity as the sons of God (vv. 26, 27), and His presence in our hearts is the promise of the total transformation that awaits us when our bodies are invested with immortality by His quickening power (vv. 11, 23). Thus our Christian life from its inception to its culmination is dependent on the Spirit.

Furthermore, the Spirit-filled church suggests a community of people who *are* Spirit-filled. Beyond what might be called the Spirit's general work in regeneration and sanctification there lies what might be called a third dimension—the enduement with power. This is not in any way to belittle the truly wonderful work of the Spirit in our new birth and spiritual development, for nothing can ever detract from this, nor is it to suggest, as some have implied, that the Spirit-filled believer is *in himself* a type superior to other Christians, a cut above the average. It is rather a recognition that, both in its teaching and its description of the spiritual life of the Early Church, the New Testament shows that there are tremendous spiritual opportunities that should be explored and experienced, not merely for their own sakes, but in order that the full purpose of God for the Church might be realized.

In one of his books, J. B. Phillips has reminded us that our God can be too small, that we can limit God because we have too narrow an understanding of His greatness. We must take care lest the horizons of our spiritual life are too small. Some of us need to have our maps of the Promised Land redrawn because they do not include all the territory of the New Testament. Too many Christians are living a flat, two-dimensional life when the full reality of this third spiritual dimension is open to them if only they would acknowledge its existence and seek to experience its depth.

It is difficult to read the New Testament without becoming aware of this dimension. When John the Baptist looked forward to the coming of the Spirit he described it in quite dramatic terms as a baptism in the Holy Ghost and fire (Matthew 3:11). When Christ himself spoke of the Spirit's coming He described it as "rivers of living water" (John 7:37-39), and again the language has a dramatic quality. This is no quiet, subterranean stream meandering unobtrusively in the depths of the personality, but a rising volume of spiritual water bursting forth and flowing, like the river in Ezekiel's vision, in ever-increasing depth and momentum, bringing life wherever it comes. The language is that of movement, depth, force.

One cannot read Acts 1:8 without being reminded that a spiritual dynamic is in view. The symbols used for the coming of the Spirit on the Day of Pentecost— the mighty, rushing wind and tongues of fire—suggest energy and dynamic movement. The words used in the Book of Acts to describe the coming of the Spirit imply vitality and mobility. They were all "filled" with the Holy Spirit. The Spirit "came upon" them. The Spirit "fell upon" them. The word *epipipto* used in this last quotation is also used by Luke to describe the encounter between the prodigal son and his father: the father "fell on his neck, and kissed him" (Luke 15:20). The language hardly describes some vague, inward experience, received "by faith," and without any recognizable symptoms, but rather it suggests a dynamic, often dramatic, encounter with the Spirit in which the subject is conscious of a divine embrace and is left in no doubt that he has met with God in a new way; nor would it seem from the New Testament that those present at the time were left in any doubt, either.

The Spirit-filled believer not only recognizes that he must be born of the Spirit and sanctified by the Spirit, but he also sees that he can be filled with the Spirit in such a way that he is endued with power from on high. Whether he calls this initial experience the "baptism in the Spirit" or "being filled with the Spirit" is of no great importance. The terminology is not as important as the reality which it attempts to describe. The fact is that the Spirit-filled man is conscious of a moment in his life when the work of the Spirit was intensified and began to reach new proportions within him.

He is like a man who has been standing on a hilltop enjoying the fresh air and open spaces of God's good earth, who suddenly takes in a deep breath so that his lungs are filled and his whole being becomes alive in a new way. The Spirit-filled man knows without doubt that the Holy Spirit has come upon him and he realizes that the language of the New Testament is not a rather picturesque and perhaps exaggerated description but an accurate definition in practical terms of what actually happens when a man is filled with the Spirit. He can test his own experience with the New Testament and can say, "This is that!" He discovers that he has the same symptoms and he knows, therefore, that he has an authentic New Testament experience of the Spirit (see Acts 11:15-17).

From the evidence we have in the New Testament

it is clear that the coming of the Spirit was always attended by supernatural manifestations. On three occasions (Acts 2:1; 10:44-47; 19:1-6) that evidence was speaking with other tongues. On one occasion (Acts 8:14-19), though the nature of the evidence was not specified, there was some clear indication that the Spirit had come, since Simon "saw" that the Holy Spirit was given. On the other occasion (Acts 9:17), although no specific manifestation is mentioned, it is not without significance that the man who was the subject of the experience could later testify that he spoke with tongues in great measure (1 Corinthians 14:18).

It would seem fair to say, therefore, that in the New Testament the normal evidence of the Spirit's coming was speaking with tongues. We have to face the fact that the only data we have for the coming of the Spirit include this strong emphasis on external evidence. If we are to be honest with Scriptures we must ask ourselves whether our experience conforms to the New Testament, or whether we are trying to adapt New Testament language to the limitations of our own experience. Are we trying to say, "That must be this," or can we honestly say, "This *is* that"? In this matter, as in all others, we cannot afford to make our experience the test of New Testament language. The only safe way is to allow the New Testament to judge our experience. The Spirit-filled man can face Paul's searching question, "Have ye received the Holy Ghost?" and humbly but honestly say, "Yes, I have—and I know it because New Testament experience has been reproduced in my life."

Even in the Early Church there were those who had not received the fullness of the Spirit. When the apostles laid down the qualifications of the first "deacons" (Acts 6:3), they were careful to specify that such men were to be "of good repute, full of the Spirit and of wisdom" (RSV). If every member of that church had been automatically Spirit-filled at conversion, there would be no need to lay down that stipulation, a fact which should remind us that, although the promise of the Spirit is given to every believer, only those who recognize that fact and humbly seek to be filled with the Spirit actually receive the promise. In this sense, the gift of the Spirit refers not to the new birth, but to the enduement with power.

One of our problems in relation to the work of the Spirit is our almost irrepressible desire to fit everything into neat categories. Bishop J. C. Ryle once observed that "men may be more systematic in their statements than the Bible," and nowhere is this more true than in the doctrine of the Spirit. God is not the author of confusion, but we must never try to imprison Him in our rigid systems of thought. It is impossible to define exactly how and where the work of the Spirit in sanctification differs from the baptism in the Spirit, the enduement with power. Certainly the latter experience results in a new enabling for service and witnessing, but it also interpenetrates the work of the Spirit at other levels.

To receive the Spirit in this sense is not only to be given power for service, but also to enter into a deeper, more intimate relationship with a divine person. There is a danger that the very language we use—wind, water, fire—can make us forget the intensely personal realities of the Pentecostal experience. We are not merely receiving power, but a person. We are not merely dealing with a source of energy, but with the Comforter. This involves us in personal relationships with Him.

This being so, it follows that the Spirit-filled man will be marked not only by the effectiveness of his work and witness, but also by the quality of his personal life. This is where the "power for service" complex is dangerous, because it tends to overlook the fact that God is as much, if not more, concerned with what we *are* as with what we *do*. If the baptism in the Spirit is an intensification of His presence and power within us, then it ought to lead not only to a more effective ministry, but also to a better quality of life.

The life that is filled with the Spirit must surely develop both a love for the Word of God and a growing understanding of it. The Spirit-filled man will thirst for truth, and this will be evidenced by his private study of the Scriptures and by his attendance at meetings for Bible study. Furthermore, such an in-depth encounter with the Spirit of Truth must inevitably lead a man away from the erroneous doctrines which he may have held hitherto. The Lord Jesus put a strong emphasis on this educative aspect of the Spirit's ministry (John 14:16, 17; 15:26; 16:13-15), and this must be the standard by which modern Pentecost must allow itself to be judged. Where there is an impatience with doctrine, a reluctance to examine the Scriptures, or an easygoing attitude to doctrinal standards in relationship to theological belief, it must be questioned whether the so-called "Pentecostal experience" is genuine. The Spirit-filled man can never be indifferent to Truth.

The baptism in the Spirit is also an in-depth encounter with the Spirit of Holiness. We have become so used to the prefix "Holy" that we have almost lost sight of its implications in relation to the person of the Spirit. It is not a handle to His name, but a description of His essential being. Perhaps one of the reasons for the shattering experience in the life of the Early Church, the death of Ananias and Sapphira, was to remind the Church that in the glory of the Pentecostal blessing we are not dealing merely with supernatural

44

phenomena, but with the Spirit of the Lord who is unspeakably holy. The fire of Pentecost is part of that consuming fire which expresses the moral glory of God. Where that fire burns, holiness must result.

Holiness is not a condition for receiving the baptism in the Spirit. The only conditions are those which pertain to all the gifts of grace, namely, faith in the promise and a desire to receive, coupled with a willingness to seek until one finds. The gift of the Spirit is no more a reward for personal virtue than is salvation. On the other hand, if one is to have an in-depth relationship with the Spirit of holiness, obviously one must be willing to be made holy. Holiness is the inevitable result of such a relationship.

The Spirit-filled man will be a holy man, but his holiness will correspond to the ideals of the Spirit and not to the taboos of men. Too often our ideas of holiness are negative and consist only of the things that ought not to be done, whereas true Biblical holiness has a strong positive content. It is not merely the avoidance of certain inward attitudes and outward acts, but the presence of a passionate love for the things which God loves. "Thou lovest righteousness, and hatest wickedness" is the Psalmist's description of the holiness of Christ (Psalm 45:7), and this emphasizes the positive as well as the negative aspects of holiness.

The priest on the Jericho road may well have preserved his ceremonial purity by refusing contact with the bloodstained victim, but his neglect of a positive concern for his fellowman stained his life far more deeply than any outward defilement could have done. It is not enough that we merely avoid outward *worldliness;* holiness must be seen as much in what we *do* as in what we *do not* do.

We must not forget, however, that holiness does involve a definite attitude towards sin and worldliness.

Even those who manifest the gifts of the Spirit may not be above criticism on this point. Unless our lives at home and in business manifest purity and integrity, our experience of the Spirit is not very deep. "Does a spring pour forth from the same opening fresh water and brackish? Can a fig tree, my brethren, yield olives, or a grapevine figs? No more can salt water yield fresh" (James 3:11, 12, RSV). By the same tokens, can the lips that have poured forth interpretation of tongues or prophecy at 11:55 on a Sunday morning snap in impatience at 1:15 p.m. the same day because of a delayed lunch?

Whatever is inconsistent with the Spirit of Holiness, whatever in thought, word, or deed would grieve Him or quench His fire in our hearts, must be brought in penitence and humble confession before Him. This holiness must touch every part of our lives, at home, in business, in the church, in our social relationships, our recreations, and our innermost beings. The power of the Spirit is expressed as much in the dynamic of a holy life as in the demonstration of spiritual gifts.

The Spirit-filled Chrisian is loyal to his church and faithful in the fulfillment of his duties in its fellowship and activities. He remains loyal even when someone else is chosen for the task he felt he could have done. He is faithful in his giving and consistent in his attendance at the meetings. His personal relationships, both in the church and outside, manifest the loving graciousness of the Lord Jesus himself. It is no accident that 1 Corinthians 13, with its beautiful description of love, is placed where it is in Paul's letter, between two chapters on spiritual gifts. It is there to remind us, not that love makes the gifts obsolete, but that love is the cement that holds the whole structure of Pentecostal life and worship together. Only when the love of God is shed abroad in our hearts by the Holy Spirit does a true Pentecostal atmosphere become possible.

The truly Spirit-filled man is not merely one who 30 years ago had an experience, but a man who today has opened his innermost being to the deep flowing river of God, a man who on bended knee with the open Word of God before him has communed afresh with God and experienced a new anointing of the Spirit of God.

It is not merely a question of speaking in tongues every day in one's private devotions, or of participating regularly in the exercise of spiritual gifts in the services. It is also allowing the Holy Spirit access to every part of our lives so that His truth, holiness, and love penetrate our whole being and flow out from us into the home, the church, and the world.

The Spirit-filled man is a man filled with the life of God, and such a man has an unmistakable spiritual vitality about him. Imagine a church full of people of this caliber. Picture the joyous spontaneity that must characterize their worship, the boundless enthusiasm of their service for the Lord, the openhearted generosity, and the warm, glowing fellowship that must make itself felt in any such community.

Are we this kind of member, or do we need spiritual renewal? If so, we need to pray: "Lord, pour out Thy Spirit on me, so that I may be Pentecostal by experience as well as by name." The answer will not be far away, for "the promise is unto you, and to your children, and to all that are afar off, even as many as the Lord our God shall call."

6

Its Fellowship

Someone has well said that "the Bible knows nothing of solitary religion," and it is true indeed that the New Testament builds its whole idea of true Christianity on the concept of corporate fellowship.

As we have seen already, the New Testament uses illustrations which cannot be understood in any other way than that the Church is to be a living community of people gathered together for a specific purpose. The Church is a building, not a collection of stones. The Church is a body, living, moving, and having its being in the uniting fellowship of the Spirit. The Church is the living vine in which every branch is united to its fellow and to the stem, and therefore has the possibility of fruitfulness.

Whether we like it or not, we are involved in the life of the Church. For practical purposes this means the local church or assembly.

It is worth noting that the Early Church devoted itself not only to the apostles' doctrine, but also to this matter of fellowship: "They continued steadfastly in . . . fellowship" (Acts 2:42). They recognized that their fellowship needed as much thought and attention as their knowledge of the faith, and therefore they gave themselves to it with the same earnestness. Their fellowship was not haphazard but positive, meaningful, and greatly enriching.

It is important to recognize the basis on which the fellowship of the Early Church was founded. Who were the people who continued steadfastly in fellowship? "They that gladly received his word." Verse 44 confirms this: "And all that believed were together." They were together because they believed certain things, because they had gladly received the word of the gospel. Their fellowship was not based on any purely human ground at all. They were not together because they shared similar political views, or came from a similar social background; nor were they members of the Church because it offered certain aesthetic attractions—like lovely architecture or inspiring music—or because of its recreational pursuits; they were there because they believed the gospel, because they had repented of sin and turned in faith to Christ. In turning to Him they found themselves inextricably bound up with each other.

We have only to glance at verses 9-11 to realize that these first Christians, though mostly Jews, came from many different parts, spoke many different dialects, and were influenced by many different cultures, but these natural differences were bridged by the grace of God in Christ. As the Church grew, the racial, social, and cultural differences between Christians widened, but the same unifying principle was at work. Thus Paul wrote to the Galatians about the natural differences which ordinarily would be divisive, but he pointed out that in Christ "there is neither Jew nor Greek, there is neither bond nor free, there is neither male nor female" (Galatians 3:28). To the Ephesians he likewise showed that Christ's work on the cross achieved reconciliation not only between God and man, but also between man and man, so that the great religious divide between Jew and Gentile was finally spanned: "For he is our peace, who hath made both one, and hath broken down the middle wall of partition between us" (Ephesians 2:14).

It would be unrealistic to ignore other lesser reasons for fellowship. Within the overall unity of the faith there are undoubted varieties of form and emphasis. For some, that faith is most meaningfully expressed in the beauties of some ancient liturgy, while for others the sounding brass of the local Salvation Army citadel is far more evocative. Obviously differences of temperament and of social background are bound to influence our choice of a particular assembly or church. In some churches we feel much more at home than in others, and this is to be expected. For the Spirit-filled believer this becomes even more important. The man who has known something of the joyous spontaneity of the Spirit in his own soul must find a fellowship where that spontaneity can find true expression. This is not to say that he regards himself as superior to other Christians. It is just that the very nature of his own spiritual experience demands a suitable environment. "We have piped unto you, and ye have not danced; we have mourned unto you, and ye have not lamented," was the complaint of the Lord Jesus against the unresponsiveness of His contemporaries. This referred to their failure to react to His preaching, but it also expressed the deep frustration which is experienced when any man finds himself in a community which is not moved by the things which stir his own heart.

"Can two walk together, except they be agreed?" asked Amos (3:3). The answer is obvious, and we would be foolish if we did not recognize that, even within the unity of believers, there are practical details which are bound to affect fellowship. It is imperative that the fellowship which we share at local and personal levels provide the necessary opportunities in which we can both contribute what we have to give, and receive what we need for our own spiritual growth.

When we have said all this, however, we must be alert to the dangers of allowing minor issues to determine our approach to the question. For some people the social prestige of belonging to a popular church is of more importance in their choice of fellowship than anything else, while for others the spiritual or intellectual image of being known as a member of a well-known preacher's congregation carries a great deal of weight. Some people leave an assembly because, so they say, of its lack of freedom, when, if the truth were known, it is because the good order of that church prevents their asserting the personal dominance they wish to have.

Why do we seek fellowship with a particular group? Why in some cases do we withdraw from fellowship? In these days of fragmentation, of groups meeting for this purpose and societies being formed for that, when all kinds of invitations are open to us and demands for support made upon us, we need to make sure that we regard this matter of fellowship as seriously as the Early Church did. Our fellowship should be based on the genuine grounds of mutual dependence on and love for Christ. Let us see it as something that demands loyalty, patience, and prayerful perseverance if it is to become meaningful and fruitful.

The implications of true Christian fellowship are tremendous. Our failure to read them into our local situation sometimes causes our restlessness. We think of our assembly or church and too often we see it as a number of people meeting together in a building of a certain shape and condition. The format of the meetings is mostly a known quantity, and the imperfections of preacher and congregation sometimes are only too obvious. With a sigh we remember the church we

51

visited on holiday or the newspaper reports of the latest spiritual movement in some distant part of the world. The scent of those greener pastures makes us dissatisfied, even impatient, with the shortcomings we see so near at home. We must never become satisfied with anything less than God's best or complacent about our true spiritual condition as an assembly, but we must not reject the fellowship in which God has placed us because in its present condition it does not measure up to our ideals.

The point we must never forget is that our assembly, if its terms of membership are anywhere near New Testament standards, is an assembly of God's children, and because of this the implications of its fellowship must not be measured by purely outward or visible standards. "That ye also may have fellowship with us," wrote John, "and truly our fellowship is with the Father, and with his Son Jesus Christ" (1 John 1:3). Fellowship with the people of God takes us into the glorious heights and depths of the very intimacy of the Godhead; it is, as Paul puts it in 2 Corinthians 13:14, the "fellowship of the Holy Ghost," and it is the fulfillment of the Lord's own prayer before He died: "That they all may be one; as thou, Father, art in me, and I in thee, that they also may be one in us" (John 17:21). True fellowship takes a community of believers into the intimate depths of divine relationships.

This fellowship transcends time and space. We love to sing that great old hymn "We're marching to Zion," but, while it expresses a great truth about our Christian hope, from another point of view it is not quite true. The fact is that we have already arrived! The writer to the Hebrews makes it clear when he says: "But ye *are come* unto mount Zion." In the succeeding verses (Hebrews 12:22-24) he goes on to show that our fellowship takes us immediately into the heavenly Jerusalem and links us with a host of angels, the "full concourse and assembly of the first-born citizens of heaven" (NEB), with God himself, with the Lord Jesus, and with those who have reached the end of their pilgrimage and are "made perfect."

Think of the implications of this. We may meet in a back street hall with a group of very ordinary people, singing hymns to the accompaniment of a wheezy organ, but if we have genuinely come to meet with God, then the external circumstances are of little account. This is not to say that we should be content with drabness or be slipshod in our approach to the more material aspects of our church life, far from it; but it is to say that the shape or size of the building, the social status of the people, or the abilities of the preacher should not cause us to denigrate the true worth of any congregation. Our fellowship takes us beyond time and space and links us with angels and the stalwarts of the faith; it leaps all known geographical barriers and takes us beyond the frontiers of our environment into the timeless, limitless fellowship of the heavenly places. Walls and roof have no significance, and oceans and political frontiers are irrelevant, for prayer leaps continents, worship encompasses constellations, faith "runs up with joy the shining way to meet its dearest Lord."

Such a fellowship puts a new value on the people who belong to it. The man next to me may be a bank director or a trash collector, but, under the terms of this fellowship, these social and economic factors do not alter the fact that, if they are regenerate, they can each be described as "the brother for whom Christ died" (1 Corinthians 8:11). This puts a supreme value on each of them. Their respective contributions to the life of the church may vary considerably, but they are both of great worth in the sight of God because they have both been purchased by the blood of His dear Son. This great truth moves Paul to say, "From now on, therefore, we regard no one from a human point of view" (2 Corinthians 5:16, RSV). Is it not time that we looked at each other in a different light? Is it not time that we saw the truth about our fellowship? Would not our approach to the meetings of the church be different if we looked past the familiar furnishings and the equally familiar faces and realized that there were angels in the meeting, that this was a microcosm of heaven, that these familiar people were the blood-bought sons of God? Do we value each other as God values us? Do we recognize the true dignity of every child of God? We may not always agree with our brother and we may not like the way he sings, but let us never forget that anyone who is good enough to worship in this company of angels should be good enough company for us as well. This is how God looks at him.

Nowhere is the solidarity of true fellowship more eloquently expressed than in the breaking of bread. Acts 2:42 reminds us that here the Early Church found one of the most satisfying ways of realizing its fellowship and, even when growing numbers made it necessary for the believers to meet in small units in homes, the breaking of bread still provided the focal point of their unity in Christ (v. 46).

The simple symbolism of the Communion service not only testified to their common dependence on the death of Christ, but also spoke of their organic unity as the body of Christ. They broke bread in remembrance of Him and at the same time they proclaimed His death and the hope of His coming (1 Corinthians 11:23-26); but they also confessed that they, being many, were "one bread and one body" (1 Corinthians 10:16, 17).

Thus, for New Testament Christians, the Communion service was not simply a memorial of the Lord's death, but an affirmation of their fellowship in Him. This gave added point to Paul's words about "not discerning the Lord's body" (1 Corinthians 11:29), for the phrase is capable of double interpretation. It may well mean the body represented by the bread—that is, the body offered on Calvary—but it may also mean the body which is composed by His Church. One thing is certain: it is impossible rightly to discern or to take into account the true value of the atoning death of Christ and at the same time to ignore the implications of fellowship with our fellow members of His body.

To partake of the Lord's Supper and to be at cross-purposes with another member of the assembly is a contradiction. The death that unites us to Christ unites us to His Church and, if we are members of Christ, then inescapably we are "members one of another" (Romans 12:5). It is not only our secret sins that bring on us the chastening of the Lord, but the sins of broken fellowship, our impatience, our whispered criticisms, our thoughtlessness, and our uneasy avoidance of each other. These are as grieving to the Lord as the more obvious sins of the flesh.

The fellowship of a Spirit-filled Church must be more than a nice idea. It must find its expression, not only in a symbolic act at the Communion service, but also in the practical day-to-day terms of living, worshiping, and working together as a community. Too often the word "fellowship" stands for a kind of spiritual heat haze, a benevolent but blurred feeling of general kindliness which disappears when the figures in the mist suddenly take on real, and sometimes awkward, shapes. In the New Testament Church, fellowship was much more than this; it was tackled with typical zest and good sense. Contrary to some modern trends, they did not abandon what we might call the total fellowship of a central gathering, but they continued, despite growing numbers, to meet together "in the temple." At the same time they recognized the importance of fellowship in smaller groups and developed the practice of meeting "from house to house" (Acts 2:46). This was no either/or situation: the smaller meetings were obviously complementary to the larger ones, and the larger meetings provided the focus for the smaller ones. In this way they avoided the dangers of fragmentation and provided opportunities for fellowship at a helpfully intimate level, a pattern which the modern Church needs to recognize and from which it must learn.

It is clear that New Testament fellowship placed a strong emphasis on spiritual things. As we have already seen, instruction in the apostles' doctrine and participation in breaking of bread figured prominently in their program. In addition Luke tells us that prayer was also one of their major fellowship activities (Acts 2:42).

As we shall see in a later chapter, worship also played an important part in their communal life. The Early Church was born in an atmosphere of earnest prayer (Acts 1:14), and prayer remained a vital part of their fellowship (Acts 3:1; 4:24; 6:4-6; 8:15; 12:5, 12; 13:3, to cite but a few instances of communal praying). It is well for us to remember that the only way in which a Spirit-filled man can remain in that condition is for him continually to seek the face of God in prayer, and that the only way for a Spirit-filled church to maintain its true Pentecostal condition is for its members to come together to meet the Lord in prayer and the ministry of His Word. There is no substitute for these. The omnipresent Lord has promised that He will concentrate His presence where two or three are gathered together in His name and, unless the local church gathers to meet her Lord in this intensely personal and spiritual sense, all her other activities will be robbed of their true vitality and power.

The Spirit-filled Church is not only an audience, but a group of participants, and as such it must be willing, individually and collectively, to "hear what the Spirit saith unto the church" and make a personal and collective response. This may involve serious decision making by the leaders of the assembly—the abandonment of former policies, or the alteration of plans already made, or the courageous initiative of a new undertaking—and it may mean drastic adjustments in the personal lives of the members, but the Spirit-filled Church will be ready for this dynamic encounter with her living Head. Our Bible studies must be more than excursions round the Biblical lighthouse and back: they must always be a confrontation with divine truth. Our prayer meetings must be more than a repeat performance for the same few voices saying the same old things; they must be an exposure of the gathered church to the presence of God through the Spirit.

Fellowship in the Spirit-filled Church can never be confined to mere meetings. Though there is fellowship in singing hymns together and listening to the Word of God, true fellowship must run more deeply than this. Too often we equate fellowship with sitting in rows in a "consecrated" building going through certain "spiritual" activities, whereas in the New Testament it was far less formal. It is clear from Acts 2:46 and from such Scriptures as 1 Corinthians 11 that the Early Church met together either in their homes or in some central place for relaxed fellowship over a meal together. Often, it would seem, the early Communion services took place in connection with a meal, or "love feast," as they were called. The practice sometimes led, as in

Corinth, to difficulties through abuse, but the basic idea was a good one. Maybe in our penchant for "meetings" we have lost the value of this social togetherness, where in our church or in our homes we can get together and talk in a completely relaxed atmosphere.

It is absolutely vital that we do not allow house fellowships to become substitutes for the church meetings. Where this happens, effective witness of the local church is seriously damaged. The smaller group must recognize its responsibility to the local church, and should be humble enough to function under the direction of and for the benefit of the assembly as a whole. It will be wise for its leadership to be appointed by the assembly and for its activities to be part of the recognized program of the church. Unless proper safeguards are provided, the smaller group grows away from the local assembly and more often than not it becomes a separate entity with little interest other than preserving its own existence.

We should also remember that fellowship must go beyond what might be called natural boundaries, it must reach past the natural affinities of age-groups, temperaments, or social backgrounds. The truly Pentecostal Church is a community in which "all flesh" is caught up in the momentum of the Spirit: sons and daughters prophesy, young men see visions, old men dream dreams, menservants and maidservants experience the outpouring of the Spirit (Acts 2:17, 18), and thus the barriers of age, sex, and social status are forgotten.

There is no place in the truly Spirit-filled church for the in-group, nor must the natural divisions between young and old be allowed to assert themselves. The Sunday school ought never to be thought of as a thing apart from the local church. The youth group or women's fellowship must never be allowed to grow away from the total fellowship of the assembly. Leaders of these groups along with the leadership of the assembly must prayerfully and practically seek to integrate them into the life of the assembly as a whole. Especially must the division between young people and older people be watched. This will call for patience and understanding on the part of those who are older, but it will also call for respect on the part of the young people and their leaders (1 Peter 5:5).

Another thing: the first Pentecostal Church manifested a great concern for the social and material well-being of its members, as well as for their spiritual needs. Theirs may have been special circumstances, but the principle of caring and sharing is an abiding one. "There was not a needy person among them," Luke tells us (Acts 4:34 RSV). He goes on to show how provision was made for widows (Acts 6:1-6) and distressed brethren (11:27-29). Dorcas is commended for her practical ministry to the poor of Lydda (Acts 9:36-39), while James defines "pure religion" in the following down-to-earth terms: "To visit the fatherless and widows in their affliction, and to keep himself unspotted from the world" (James 1:27; 2:15, 16). Paul urges the Romans to "contribute to the needs of the saints" (12:13, RSV) and lays down well-defined principles for the sharing of material benefits among Christians (1 Timothy 5:3-16), stressing that assistance should be given only where it is genuinely needed and underlining that Christian families should accept responsibility for their own relatives (vv. 8, 16).

The fellowship of the Spirit-filled church must be truly spiritual, but intensely practical. It certainly means worshiping and praying together, but it also means working together and bearing one another's burdens. It means fellowship in evangelism (Philippians 1:5), but it also means fellowship in sharing needs. It means that our total resources—spiritual, intellectual, emotional, and material—are at the disposal of the body of Christ. It means more than fine words; it means a genuine concern and willingness to help the "brother for whom Christ died."

7

Its Ministry

Perhaps the most significant moment in the dramatic story of Ezekiel's visit to the valley of dry bones (Ezekiel 37:1-10) is the moment when he is commanded to "prophesy unto the wind." He has previously spoken the words which God commanded him and has seen the effect of that prophecy on the scattered bones: they have been brought together, "bone to his bone," and clothed with flesh, a truly remarkable demonstration of the power of the word of God. At this point Ezekiel is commanded to prophesy again, this time to the wind, calling for the breath of God to come upon these slain that they might live. As he does so, the wind of God moves over the vast host of inert bodies and they live and stand upon their feet, an "exceeding great army." The whole story is a magnificent demonstration of the fact that revival can be brought about only by the Word of God and the Spirit of God.

For us, however, the story illustrates another important principle because it discloses an important sequence of events in the process of renewal. If you read the story carefully you will see that there is a sequence of life towards movement, of union towards function. It is not enough that the bones have come together; the story demonstrates that of itself unity can be a dead thing. God is concerned with more than unity; He demands life. With the coming of life, however, there is also movement—as the Spirit of God enters them they stand upon their feet. The Spirit galvanizes union into function, and the hitherto dry bones are welded into a living, moving army with tremendous potential.

All this illustrates something the Church must never forget. Unity is important, but, unless it is a unity of life and action, it has little relevance. Unless the body of Christ lives and *moves* it cannot have its being in the fullest sense. Without meaningful activity it is at best an invalid; at worst, a corpse. Unless the building of God has a function, it is nothing more than a kind of spiritual "folly," an interesting but useless extravagance; or at worst, a ruin. Unless the bride of Christ responds in loving obedience to the will of her Lord and Saviour, the relationship between them is one not of fruitful union, but of frustrating coexistence.

The ideas lying behind New Testament "church-language" do not content themselves, therefore, with unity alone but with unity leading to action—in a word, with ministry; and the idea of ministry is not confined to a special class, but embraces every member. In Paul's repeated use of the body as a type of the Church, he constantly stresses the fact that every member is important to the whole: "the eye cannot say to the hand, I have no need of thee: nor again the head to the feet, I have no need of you" (1 Corinthians 12:21). There may be a variety of form and function, but there is also a unity of interdependence in which the body grows by that which every part supplies (Ephesians 4:16).

Ezekiel's vision reminds us that when the Spirit comes there is not only life, but movement—and movement which has the disciplined cohesion of an army on the march. Gibbon the historian has described the whirling dervishes of the desert in a very telling phrase: "They mistook the giddiness of the head for the illumination of the Spirit." When we talk of life and movement, we must never forget that what the Spirit brings is not simply a sensation or a subjective experience which has its end in itself, but is a quickening of spiritual life which will result in a meaningful contribution to the life of the Church as a whole. The Pentecostal Movement has often suffered, in practical ways as well as in reputation, from the activities of those who seem only to be interested in the supernatural for its own sake. There are always those who hunger for experiences and reject experience, who opt out of the life and disciplines of the local church in order that they may enjoy the "closed shop" of small private meetings where they can indulge their appetites for the unusual. To such people any idea of church order is unacceptable because it inevitably means "quenching the Spirit"! They are therefore unwilling to commit themselves to any assembly because they fear that this would be a loss of "liberty." The Spirit-filled Church, however, must submit to the standards of the New Testament. In doing so it is bound to recognize that the Holy Spirit has come, not merely to give us supernatural phenomena but to forge us into a living, meaningful community of people who, for all our weaknesses and failures are functioning as the body of Christ in terms of growth and ministry.

The Spirit-filled Church is not a collection of people who, for all our weaknesses and failures, are but is a fellowship of believers who are sharing in the life of the Spirit because they have opened themselves completely to Him and are allowing Him to work increasingly within their own lives and at the same time to draw them into a closer relationship with each other. In the terms of this fellowship they recognize the lordship of Christ, not as an abstract ideal, but as the practical basis of their common life. They recognize that, if they are truly members of His body, then He must be their Head in a very real sense. To them, this teaching of the New Testament about the body of Christ is not merely picture language, but a statement of a vital principle. Their constant endeavor is to find out what this really means for them as a fellowship and then to work it out in practical ways.

It follows that, if the Church is the body of Christ, she is the instrument of His purpose. In other words, she exists for His sake, not merely for her own. Thus all the activities of the local church ought to be the practical expression of His will, not merely the product of someone's bright ideas. It is important that all who are engaged in the work of the local assembly seek to know what the will of God is. This means that the pastor's study (or its modern version, "office"), the deacons' meeting, the Sunday school teachers' meeting, the youth workers' discussion, the outreach teams' planning session and every other place where policies are decided must be a place where "prayer is wont to be made." I do not mean the perfunctory opening gambit, "Will Brother Jones commit us to the Lord, please," but a definite opening of hearts and minds to the Lord which commences even before the meeting begins. Out of such a meeting the first missionary enterprise of the Church was born (Acts 13:2). Such a heart-attitude dominated the thinking of the Church's greatest theologian-evangelist (Acts 9:6). Unless the Body obeys the Head it can never become the "fulness of him that filleth all in all" (Ephesians 1:23).

When we define the ministry of the Spirit-filled

Church there are two extremes that must be avoided.

On the one hand, there is what we might call "minister-centeredness." This, while it pays lip service to the priesthood of all believers, tends to feel that anything that is not done by a properly trained and usually full-time minister is not "official." It has the severe disadvantage of turning the minister into an ungainly one-man band, while relegating everyone else to "amateur" status: "He's very good, but of course he's never had any training. . . ." No one who has heard the call to the ministry will deny the solemn yet glorious reality of that call, but no one who understands the nature of the Church will believe for a moment that God vested everything in the full-time ministry.

On the other hand, there is the danger of what we might call "free-for-allness." While it pays lip service to New Testament teaching about the body of Christ and makes a great play on what it calls "body ministry," it tends to reject the very principle on which a body depends; namely, orderly arrangement and controlled function. While it properly recognizes the equality of believers as far as their personal standing before God is concerned, it tends to overlook the fact that God has not made everyone equal as far as their function is concerned. He has "set some in the church" to fulfill ministries which are of a higher order than others (1 Corinthians 12:28-30), and within that divinely given order He has provided for leadership, discipleship, and a rich variety of ministry.

The one extreme leads to overworked professionalism, the other to spiritual anarchy. Both are a denial of New Testament standards.

In the New Testament the work of the ministry is variously described. In this chapter we shall look at several areas in which it occurs.

The Early Church placed a strong emphasis on *the ministry of the Word.* The apostles were determined that nothing, however important, should be allowed to interfere with this aspect of their ministry. "It is not reason," they said, "that we should leave the word of God, and serve tables" (Acts 6:2). They eased the pressures on themselves by appointing others to do what they considered to be lesser duties. Perhaps the early disciples were so eager to "continue steadfastly in the apostles' doctrine" because the apostles were so eager to "give themselves to prayer and the ministry of the word."

The complaint that people are no longer interested in Bible study may be due as much to the superficial preparation of the preacher as to the fickleness of the congregation. Certainly the first Pentecostal Church put the ministry of the Word high on its list of priorities. In his Letters to young ministers Paul constantly urged them to give themselves to the study and exposition of the Word of God (1 Timothy 4:6, 13-16; 2 Timothy 4:1-5; Titus 2:1), and in his First Letter to Timothy (5:17) he went so far as to advise that the elder who specialized "in the word and doctrine" was worthy of "double honor," a term which contains the idea of financial support. This in itself is an indication of the supreme value put on the ministry of the Word by the first Christians.

The reason is not far to seek. The ministry of the Word was the spearhead of evangelism. In a society which, like ours, had succumbed to the errors of man, myth, and magic, only the proclamation of the gospel could penetrate the ramifications of falsehood, and open blind eyes. Against a background of blind paganism staggering drunkenly along the cliff edge of coming judgment, Paul urged Timothy to "do the work of an evangelist," and that work clearly was defined in the words: "Preach the word, be urgent in season and out of season, convince, rebuke, and exhort, be unfailing in patience and in teaching" (2 Timothy 4:2, RSV). The basic elements of good preaching are underlined here, and the modern preacher of the gospel will do well to give careful consideration to every word of this injunction. He will also do well to study the sermons recorded in the Book of Acts, for he will be reminded that true Pentecostal preaching is no slaphappy, "open-your-mouth-wide-and-I-will-fill-it" ranting, but prayerful, careful exposition of Scripture in which arguments are brought to bear on the minds and hearts of the listeners. They are the words of men who have clearly "given themselves" to prayer and to the ministry of the Word. There is no modern substitute.

The ministry of the Word is basic to the true growth of the Church. In this way the flock of God is fed, nourished, and protected from the evil influences of false doctrines. In his moving farewell to the leaders of the Ephesian Church, Paul warns them of the dangers that will beset them both from without and within their fellowship, but then he points them to the secret of successful growth: "And now, brethren, I commend you to God, and to the word of his grace, which is able to build you up" (Acts 20:32). He has learned that the Word of God, understood, expounded, and obeyed, is the only real defense against error and the only soil in which true faith can flourish. This is why he urges Timothy to study to show himself a workman approved unto God (2 Timothy 2:15) and tells Titus to appoint elders who "hold firm to the sure word as taught" so that they are able to "give instruction in sound doctrine and also to confute those who contradict it" (Titus 1:9, RSV).

The seriousness with which the New Testament

views the ministry of the Word is a challenge to us and a rebuke to the superficial way in which we sometimes approach it. We who are pastors and teachers are sometimes guilty of failing to delegate to others work which they could well do, with the result that we do not have sufficient time to give ourselves to prayer and the ministry of the Word. We like to see ourselves as good all-rounders—men who can do everything that needs to be done—and we often end up by doing it. It is certainly right for us to be practical men, able when necessity requires it to put our hand to anything, but it is a contradiction of good sense (Exodus 18:14-23) and of the scriptural doctrine of the Church to insist on doing everything ourselves when others are both capable and willing to share in the ministry.

Sometimes congregations are at fault in this, because they insist on "having the minister" when someone else would have done just as well, if not better. We seem to suffer under the illusion that the call to the ministry automatically enables a man to be better at everything than anyone else, and our tendency towards minister-centered churches sometimes results in the failure to recognize the full spectrum of ministry-potential among us. There are those among us who have a gift for exposition or for evangelism who, though they have not felt the call to a full-time ministry, could nevertheless supplement the work of the pastor, whose ministry gifts may lie in other directions. We need to pray for the gift of recognizing the true potential in our churches, and for the grace to give opportunity for it to be exercised.

Obviously there are problems here. There are always those who wrongly imagine they "have a ministry," and there are those for whom access to the pulpit would give them the preeminence they covet. But, for all this, we need to look for the genuine gifts that God has given to His Church and provide opportunities for their use. Above all, those who are called to handle the Word of God must give themselves to this ministry with prayerful, devoted study, refusing to allow lesser things to distract them from this supreme task. As Pentecostal people we must see that the ministry of the Word is given its right place both in the time we allot to it in our weekly program and the undivided attention we give to it when it is proclaimed.

The ministry of leadership also dominated the thinking of the Early Church. Whether it be a family or a nation, a business or a church, every community needs good leadership. One of the worst eras in Israel's history occurred during the period of the Judges, when "every man did that which was right in his own eyes," a reminder that the freedom of the individual is only truly realized when it is related to the purpose of God for His people as a whole. This principle is clearly recognized in the teaching and practice of the New Testament, for, although it does not lay down a rigid structure of church government, it definitely indicates that responsible leadership and its corollary, loyal membership, are an essential part of normal church life.

Almost the first thing that Paul and Barnabas did on their missionary journeys was to appoint "elders in every church" (Acts 14:23). It is not my purpose to discuss in detail the definition of the various offices mentioned in the New Testament, but it is significant that the elder, or "bishop" as he is called in 1 Timothy 3:1, was a man appointed to exercise oversight and leadership in the local church.

In other words, although the Early Church recognized the equality of believers, it also recognized the need for leadership and discipline in the local assembly, and it insisted that the members of the assembly respected and obeyed that leadership so long as it was in keeping with scriptural principles (1 Thessalonians 5:12, 13; Hebrews 13:17). In our insistence on the priesthood of all believers and our rejection of the clergy/laity distinction, we must not overlook that God has set in the Church "governments" (the word is *kubernesis* and denotes a helmsman, or pilot) as well as workers of miracles and speakers in tongues (1 Corinthians 12:28). Nor must we overlook that the risen Lord's gifts to the Church include those of oversight and leadership (Ephesians 4:11 12).

The ministry of leadership requires qualifications. In the first place, there must be the enabling selection of the Holy Spirit (Acts 20:28). In the second place, there must be spiritual, moral, and domestic qualities to commend a man for this work (1 Timothy 3:1; Titus 1:5-9). The man who cannot control himself or command the respect of his own family can hardly exercise good leadership in the household of God. Leadership is not a question of giving orders, but of inspiring confidence, setting a good example, and encouraging others in the service of God. The elder may well minister the Word (1 Timothy 5:17), but he is also called to be a pastor, or shepherd of God's flock (1 Peter 5:1-4). This is a ministry which cannot be truly fulfilled by one who merely wishes to earn a living or assert his authority over others. It requires a loving heart, a dedicated life, a watchful, praying spirit, and a patient, painstaking concern for every individual placed under his care.

Leadership occurs at many levels. In the overall sense it probably lies in the pastor of the church, but not exclusively so. It is significant that more than once in the New Testament the plural, "elders," occurs, indicating that leadership was not necessarily vested in one man. Though in a general sense the term "elder" would seem to correspond with the work of what we today would call a "minister," it would be a mistake for us to feel that all spiritual leadership should be confined to this. Wherever there are mature brethren of good standing and real spirituality there is the potential of leadership, and this should be recognized and encouraged.

The Early Church appointed Stephen and Philip to be "deacons," but it did not insist that they confine themselves to the administration of funds. It recognized their wider ministry by giving them every opportunity of exercising it (Acts 6:1-6, 8; 8:5). In the same way we must learn to recognize the gifts that God has conferred among us. Our concept of the diaconate ought not to be confined to that of a group of good businessmen who can deal with church finance or the maintenance of the building. It should include men of spiritual ability who can share with the pastor in the care of souls and the oversight of the Church in every aspect of its life.

As pastors we need to learn humbly to recognize that there are others in the assembly with whom we can share spiritual leadership, and as churches we need to learn to be willing to acknowledge and trust men of obvious integrity and ability among us.

Our business meetings ought to have more than broken gutters or faulty heating systems on their agendas; they should be concerned with the total condition of the assembly. We need to see that men of ability are given responsible oversight over the various departments of the church so that they are actively involved in its missionary support, its evangelistic outreach, its youth work, the care of the elderly, and so on. This will call for trust, and it will demand not only willingness to take responsibility, but willingness to work as a well-coordinated team under the general leadership of the minister. It will also spread the burden and create a deeper sense of involvement.

There will be problems—there is nearly always a Diotrephes wanting to throw his weight about (3 John 9)—but this ought not to deter us from recognizing the value of sharing the leadership of the work. We need to be on the lookout for potential leaders and provide opportunities for their development so that with the march of time the Church is able to keep in step with the purpose of God.

The ministry of personal involvement was vital to the Early Church. There are differing opinions today over the duties undertaken by the various types of ministry referred to in the New Testament. Even a term like "helps" (1 Corinthians 12:28 is of uncertain meaning, though Charles Hodge in his commentary suggests that it means "persons qualified and appointed to help the other officers in the church, probably in the care of the poor and the sick. These according to the common understanding from Chrysostom to the present day, were deacons and deaconesses."

Whatever interpretation we may place on this word and others used in the Epistles, one thing is certain: the New Testament envisages a whole range of ministries supplementing the ministry of the Word and spiritual leadership. It expects that every member of the Church will make a personal contribution to its life and ministry and in so doing enable it to grow towards full maturity as the body of Christ (Ephesians 4:16). In Romans 12:4-13 Paul lists some of the practical ways in which members may minister one to another and contribute to the corporate life of the Church: teaching, the ministry of spiritual gifts such as prophecy, the ministry of encouragement, financial support, and practical help in various ways. There is no end to the variety of gifts among us, and there should be no end to their proper exercise. The Church needs intercessors. It needs those who will devote themselves to the care of the young and the elderly and lonely. It needs personal evangelists. It needs those who give hospitality. It needs the loving care and concern with which the members will look after each other and encourage each other.

One of the glorious privileges of the Spirit-filled Church is the possession and manifestation of the supernatural gifts of the Spirit. Indeed, it would be true to say that a Pentecostal church cannot live up to its name unless it is both coveting earnestly and exercising scripturally these great spiritual gifts.

This is not the place to discuss in detail all that is involved in the exercise of spiritual gifts, but it is necessary that we should recognize their value and their vital importance to the full ministry of the Church. It is surely significant that, even when appointing men to what was a minor administrative task—the handling of the widows' fund—the Early Church insisted that they be Spirit-filled men (Acts 6:3). This is a reminder that, in every aspect of ministry, we need not only the infilling of the Spirit, but the gifts of the Spirit as well.

It is clear from the list that Paul gives in 1 Corinthians 12:8-11 that these gifts are not Pentecostal playthings, spiritual novelties to amuse the spiritually immature, but a divine provision designed to equip the Church for her superhuman task in the world. In every local church there are normal human ministries in which the natural (though God-given) abilities of the members are employed in various ways, but God has also bestowed the gifts of the Spirit as channels through which He can decisively and effectively enter

73

into the activities of the Church at any given moment.

These gifts are not extensions of natural gifts, but expressions of the supernatural power of the Spirit: they are not intended to supplant human abilities, but to supplement them. The gift of prophecy, for instance, is not a specially eloquent type of preaching, but a direct communication of the word of God given in a supernatural way through the operation of the Holy Spirit on the person who exercises the gift. The gifts of healings are not medical skills, but the direct operation of the Holy Spirit in a given situation. Thus, in addition to the natural gifts, which the Church should gratefully recognize and seek to develop, there are supernatural gifts of the Spirit which can lift it above its natural limitations and give it a new dimension of life and effectiveness.

The Spirit-filled Church recognizes that the gifts of the Spirit are available today, and it therefore obeys the scriptural injunction to "covet earnestly the best gifts." With wonder and heartfelt thanks to God, it realizes that the word of wisdom or the word of knowledge uttered in the context of, say, a committee meeting, a sermon, or during a difficult session of personal counseling, may bring the resources of God's mind to bear on a situation with an immediacy and directness not possible in any other way. It sees, too, that prophecy (or tongues and interpretation) can likewise pour refreshing streams of inspiration and edification into a meeting, like a spring welling up from an ancient source, and it gladly listens to what the Spirit says to the Church. It realizes that divinely-given faith can unlock otherwise unknown possibilities, that the working of miracles and the gifts of healings granted by the Spirit can bring unlimited divine resources to bear upon the desperate human situation in which the Church is called to minister. It values the discerning of spirits because it is an indispensable weapon in the Church's warfare against the powers of darkness.

The truly Pentecostal church will not disparage education or the great natural gifts which God has bestowed upon its members. It will seek by prayer and diligence to employ all its powers in the service of the Lord, but at the same time it will recognize that, over and above those natural gifts, God in His superabundance has bestowed the glorious gifts of the Spirit, and in humble faith and earnest desire it will reach out to receive those gifts from the nail-pierced hands of the risen Lord. Its ministry will never be complete without them.

The ministries which God has set in the Church are many and varied, but one thing is common to them all: the true motive inspiring every ministry must be the glory of God. In the last analysis, our ministry is to Him and, because of this, what we do and how we do it must be governed by His will. Our final ambition must be to please Him who loved us and gave himself for us. Nothing else is good enough.

8

Its Worship

What a wealth of meaning is summed up in the two words that head this chapter! One can feel, even at this distance in time, the throb of life and spontaneous joy vibrating from the hearts of these men and women meeting to worship the Christ who had touched them with such grace and power. "A living church," wrote Dr. J. S. Whale, "is a worshiping, singing church; not a school of people holding all the correct doctrines." While we must never underestimate the importance of correct doctrine, neither must we forget that worship is essential to the life of the Church. Orthodoxy can be so sound that it is sound asleep. There is a kind of prim, clinical Christianity which insists on being so precise that it is almost afraid to breathe lest it utter a theological indiscretion or commit a liturgical faux pas. It reminds one of Tennyson's much lamented Maud:

"Faultily faultless, icily regular, splendidly null,
        Dead perfection, no more."

There is nothing so dead as deep-frozen religion.

Where there is real spiritual life there is bound to be spontaneous worship. The Spirit-filled church is a church which cannot resist the impulse to worship because this is the outlet for its deepest feelings and the summit of its highest aspirations. It knows, to use Peter's words, that it has been called to be "a spiritual house, a holy priesthood, to offer up spiritual sacrifices, acceptable to God by Jesus Christ" (1 Peter 2:5) or, as verse 9 of the same chapter puts it, "Ye are a chosen generation . . . that ye should show forth the praises of him who hath called you out of darkness into his marvelous light."

In a striking sentence Paul expresses this deep consciousness of the Early Church that it was called to be a worshiping community when he says to the Ephesians (1:12, RSV): "We . . . have been destined and appointed to live for the praise of His glory." This is the supreme function of every Christian and of every church. The church which fails to worship has failed to fulfill its true vocation; for, whatever else it may do in terms of evangelism or the alleviation of human need, its supreme ministry is a Godward one.

Dr. A. W. Tozer highlighted this in his little book *Worship: The Missing Jewel in the Evangelical Church.* "We're here," he says, "to be worshipers first and workers only second. We take a convert and immediately make a worker out of him. God never meant it to be so. God meant that a convert should learn to be a worshiper, and after that he can learn to be a worker."

Such words may cause some uneasiness in the ranks of evangelical activists. They touch a vital nerve. Too often we are so absorbed in what we like to call "our work for God" that we fail to catch the breathtaking vision of the holiness and glory of the Lord for whom we say we work. Like Martha, we are "distracted with much serving" and fail to make time to sit at His feet in adoring wonder.

The child Samuel, we are told in 1 Samuel 3:1, "ministered unto the Lord" in the house of God at Shiloh, but the same chapter tells us (v. 7), "Now Samuel did not yet know the Lord." It is possible to be busy in the service of God without really knowing Him, to be extremely active about the sanctuary without stopping to worship. Only the man who has seen with Isaiah "the King, the Lord of hosts" and has prostrated himself before God is really competent to say, "Here am I! Send me." The perspiring enthusiast can miss the wonder of worship as easily as the frigid formalist.

What is worship? The basic meaning of the Hebrew word for worship is "to bow oneself down." The Greek word, *proskuneo*, one of the most frequent words for worship in the New Testament, means literally "to kiss the hand toward." Both words suggest an outward action which expresses an inward realization of the greatness of the person to whom it is directed. The English word comes from an old Anglo-Saxon word which conveyed the idea of "worth-ship," that is, a recognition of the worth or value of some person or thing. In the highest sense, worship is the realization of the supreme worth of God—His utter worthiness to receive our adoration and reverent praise.

Worship is the recognition of *who He is.* Some of the finest examples of worship are found in the Book of Revelation. Straining with John to see through the door that has been opened in heaven, we catch a glimpse of the great worshiping host of angels and redeemed men and women. It soon becomes clear that the highest levels of adoration are reached when the vast company is carried away with the sheer glory of God. Like the sound of many waters, the surging tides of worship roll towards the central throne of the universe with words like these:

"Holy, holy, holy, Lord God Almighty, which was,

and is, and is to come.... Thou art worthy, O Lord, to receive glory and honor and power: for thou hast created all things, and for thy pleasure they are and were created" (Revelation 4:8-11).

"Alleluia; Salvation, and glory, and honor, and power, unto the Lord our God; for true and righteous are his judgments.... And again they said, Alleluia.... Praise our God, all ye his servants, and ye that fear him, both small and great.... Alleluia: for the Lord God omnipotent reigneth. Let us be glad and rejoice, and give honor to him" (Revelation 19:1-7).

Worship exults in the sheer glory of the Lord. It cannot help exclaiming in pure delight at the wonder it sees. Faber has caught the spirit of it in his magnificent hymn, "My God, how wonderful Thou art." He knows that true worship moves on and on, upward until it is absorbed in God himself:

> Father of Jesus, love's reward,
> What rapture will it be
> Prostrate before Thy throne to lie,
> And gaze, and gaze on Thee!

Worship is also the recognition of *what He has done*. It is difficult to separate these two ideas. Even in the great passages from the Apocalypse which we have already quoted, passages concerned with how great God is, the theme of what He has done keeps recurring, like a vast undertow to these mounting waves of worship. The hymn "For all the Lord has done for me, I never will cease to praise Him" may have a very different style from Faber's majestic meter, but its joyous gratitude is another facet of true worship. One can imagine its being sung at the Beautiful Gate of the temple by the lame man as he entered the sacred precincts, "walking, and leaping, and praising God";

79

not even Solomon's great choir, accompanied by its fanfare of trumpets, could have sounded sweeter in the ears of the Lord. In the great songs of the Revelation the theme is expressed with unparalleled beauty, as in the opening chapter for instance:

"Unto him that loved us, and washed us from our sins in his own blood, and hath made us kings and priests unto God and his Father; to him be glory and dominion for ever and ever. Amen."

The passage from Revelation 11:17 expresses sheer relief at God's intervention in a situation which otherwise was beyond control:

"We give thee thanks, O Lord God Almighty ... because thou hast taken to thee thy great power, and hast reigned."

Thus worship not only adores God for the essential glory of His being, it also praises Him for what He had done. It is the upturned face of adoring wonder, the outstretched arms of thankful love.

It would be quite wrong to think that worship is confined to the place of private communion with God or to certain occasions when the church gathers specifically for this purpose. If worship is to "show forth the praises" of God, then God is worshiped every time an evangelist sincerely preaches the gospel, for nothing shows forth His praises more than this. In the same way, God is worshiped every time a man tells his neighbor about the goodness of God. It is significant that after Peter has talked about the Church's being called to show forth the praises of God, he goes on to emphasize the importance of the believer's personal conduct in the ordinary, everyday situations of life (1 Peter 2:11-25). In other words, our behavior ought to be an act of worship, and the greater our realization of the glory of the Lord Jesus and the deeper our awareness of our indebtedness to Him, the more anxious we shall be to glorify Him at every possible opportunity (1 Corinthians 10:31).

In the same way, Christian service should be an act of worship. When Paul calls in Romans 12:1 for utter dedication to the cause of Christ, he does so on the grounds that the mercies of God demand no less a response, and he calls this response "your reasonable service," or, as the RSV renders it, "your spiritual worship." The word he uses, *latreia*, is capable of both renderings, and reminds us that the ideas of worship and service are closely woven together.

It is said that Mrs. Ruth Graham, wife of the famous evangelist, has a plaque over her kitchen sink bearing the words, "Divine service will be performed here three times a day"—a reminder that the humblest task performed in Christ's name and for His glory is an act of worship which is acceptable to Him. There ought to be no division of the Christian's life into "sacred" and "secular" compartments. The whole of life belongs to the Lord and ought to be lived with reference to His will and concern for His honor. When this happens the whole of life is lifted to a new level and made fragrant with the spirit of worship.

Yet there are times when worship is expressed in a special manner, and it is both desirable and necessary that the Church should gather for the definite purpose of praising God in a corporate way. The Lord put the seal of His approval on this when He declared that where two or three are gathered in His name, there He is in the midst. It is worth reflecting that if the omnipresent Lord of the universe has promised to "concentrate," as it were, His presence where His disciples are gathered together, He must regard it of supreme importance that they should do so. There is a tremendous value in the corporate worship of the Church. It fulfills the divine intention that the Church is the body of Christ; it manifests God's redemptive and reconciling power to the angelic hosts (see Ephesians 3:10; and notice 1 Corinthians 11:10, which suggests that angels are observers of the Church at worship); and it provides for the individual believer the stimulus of fellowship and mutual encouragement (Hebrews 10:25). If we neglect the gathering of ourselves together we rob God, we rob the Church, and we rob ourselves.

Worship is more than a matter of words, however. In His conversation with the woman at the well, Christ laid down the basic principle of worship when He declared: "God is a Spirit: and they that worship him must worship him in spirit and in truth" (John 4:24). True worship must be spiritual. It may be expressed in physical ways, in words and actions, but at its center it is a thing of the spirit. Without this spiritual center the words and actions are mere meaningless gestures.

However it is expressed externally, true worship is the spiritual deep of man's inner being, calling in response to the divine deep of God's self-revelation; it is the Godward outreach of a man's heart, mind, and spirit. Such a response can never be fully realized until a man has been filled with the Spirit of God. This is the point of Paul's words in Ephesians 5:18, 19: "Be filled with the Spirit; speaking to yourselves in psalms and hymns and spiritual songs." It is the province of the Spirit to glorify Christ, and He never does so more wonderfully than when He moves upon the Spirit of a redeemed man and enables him to worship the Lord at levels beyond his natural reach.

Spiritual worship must be in truth. To worship the Lord in the Spirit involves deep feeling, but we must never forget that it also means that we must worship Him in truth.

What does this mean? In the first place, it means that we must realize at least something of the truth about God. Christ touched on this when He said to the Samaritan woman, "Ye worship ye know not what: we know what we worship" (John 4:22). Vague feelings are not enough. Real worship is an intelligent response to the truth about God, and it results from a confrontation with the glory and grace of God as they are revealed in His Word and by His Spirit.

In the second place, it means a sincere response to the truth which has been revealed. There must be integrity as well as intelligence in our worship. Christ condemned His contemporaries because they drew near to God with their lips, but their hearts were far from Him (Matthew 15:8). This is a solemn reminder that, unless our lives correspond to the utterances of our lips, our worship is unacceptable to God. The man who climbs the hill of the Lord and stands in His holy place must have clean hands and a pure heart, because the inescapable law of the sanctuary is: "Worship the Lord in the beauty of holiness." We must never forget that "without holiness no man shall see the Lord."

However impassioned our words, however eloquent our phraseology, however beautiful our singing, however impressive our ceremonial, however spontaneous our participation in worship, unless it all comes from a sincere heart and a humble, yielded life, it will be nothing more than a hollow, discordant echo. The sensitive ear of God is more concerned to hear the tone of the heart than the timbre of the voice, and we who worship Him need to be more concerned about singing with grace in our hearts (Colossians 3:16) than about the trivialities of outward show.

Having said this, however, we would be wrong to think that the outward details of worship are unimportant. The gift itself is more important than the wrapping, but even so we usually are at pains to see that the wrapping befits the gift. Can anything less than the best be good enough for the Lord? With this in mind, it might be helpful if we thought about some of the more practical aspects of our worship.

To begin with, we need to remind ourselves again and again that every meeting is a "worship service" and every part of a meeting is "worship." Unconsciously we tend to treat our Sunday morning service as "the worship service," but, while there may be elements in this service which provide a special focus for worship, we must never regard any service or meeting as anything less than an act of worship. The prayer meeting ought to be steeped in worship and praise; the Bible study, the youth meeting, and the women's meeting ought to be times when Christ is adored; the evangelistic service ought not be be geared merely to influence men, but also to glorify God.

In the same way, we need to recognize the sacred implications of every part of a service. Every hymn ought to be an avenue down which the adoring soul walks hand in hand with God, and every prayer and every Bible reading a sweet exchange of confidence with the Lord and Lover of our souls. Every sermon, both in the preaching and the listening, should be an acknowledgement of His greatness. God save us from the scandal of "preliminaries," and help us to understand that all the time we spend in His presence should be spent in worship, even though it may be expressed in different ways.

There must be order. If worship is to please God it must correspond to His nature. When we choose a gift for anyone, we take into account what we know of his likes and dislikes, and we try to please him by giving something that will appeal to his tastes. In the same way, worship is a gift for God and it must be in keeping with His tastes. Thus Paul reminds the Corinthians, whose enthusiasm was tending to run away with them, that God is essentially a God of order (1 Corinthians 14:33) and that those who worship Him must do so in an orderly way (v. 40). The whole point of this chapter on the use of spiritual gifts is that they should be exercised in a way that will please God and enrich the life of the Church.

It is significant, however, that Paul does not seek to achieve order by the imposition of liturgical forms, but rather by an appeal to the self-discipline of the believers. Here is no cut-and-dried "order of service," but a few simple guidelines by which the individual worshiper can best serve the assembly and yet retain a sense of freedom. Thus Paul points out in verse 19 that he imposes certain restraints upon himself. He can speak with tongues more than anyone (and, contrary to some modern opinions, rejoices in the fact!), but in the assembly he deliberately restrains this facility in order that the assembly may benefit. He urges others to follow his example (v. 28).

Again, in verses 26-33, he points out that, in order to avoid confusion, certain limitations should be placed on the number of utterances through the Spirit in any one meeting, and he goes on to remind his readers that, despite the protests of some who say "I couldn't help it," a man under the anointing of the Spirit does not lose either the ability or the responsibility to maintain self-control. "The spirits of the prophets are subject to the prophets."

It becomes clear, then, that while we must preserve the precious heritage of Pentecostal liberty, we can only do so when we are willing to accept the disciplines of scriptural order, and this means the readiness on the part of every member of the assembly to act responsibly. The Spirit-filled church is not a gathering of spectators, but a company of eager participants, each of whom carries the responsibility of participating in and contributing to the act of corporate worship in a distinctly personal way. This can happen only when individually we prepare our hearts beforehand. We must come prayerfully to the house of God, and we need to spend the time before each meeting, not in exchange of idle pleasantries, but in the quiet preparation of our hearts and minds before God.

A lack of true heart preparation for worship has many side effects. It makes us insensitive to the leading of the Spirit. We become edgy and hurried, feeling that we must get things moving, so perhaps we start up choruses which are not really appropriate to the Spirit of the meeting. Our insensitivity to the Spirit of God can so easily make us mistake silence for "deadness," with the result that we feel that every moment of a service must be filled with some kind of sound. Yet there is a holy quietness which is thrillingly alive because it is brought about by the brooding of the Spirit of God, and we need to recognize and respond to those moments of rare beauty. All too often, however, they are shattered because someone gets to his feet to lead in prayer or praise, or starts the almost inevitable chorus designed to fill the gap.

Again, there are moments in a service when stillness is of particular value. For instance, immediately following an utterance in prophecy or interpretation of tongues it seems desirable that the congregation should have time for quiet reflection on what has been said through the Spirit; yet all too often the impact is lost because someone starts to sing.

It is difficult to concentrate during the time when the bread and wine are being distributed at the Communion Service if there is a constant succession of choruses. I suppose we are not all the same, but I find it much easier really to "commune" with the Lord in an atmosphere of quietness. By the same token, I find it difficult, and I imagine many others must do so, too, to give my mind to remembering the Lord's death and at the same time try to listen to the exercise of the gifts of the Spirit. It would be wrong to lay down hard and fast rules for this, but it does seem that common sense, as well as a sensitivity to the Spirit's leading, would help us avoid some of the things that sometimes detract from our worship.

A word about monopolies would not be out of place. There are some churches where the same people get up and say virtually the same things every Sunday morning, and other churches where the ministry of the gifts of the Spirit is monopolized by one or two people. "But if I don't get up, no one else will," is the self-justification made by some who are guilty of this, whereas the truth of the matter is that they would be very put out if anyone else had the temerity to encroach on their sacred preserves. It is a tragedy when worship or the exercise of spiritual gifts becomes the occasion of jealousy or self-display, yet this can and does happen and it is something about which we all need to search our hearts.

We thank God for our freedom, and for that very reason we must guard it. This puts a great responsibility on Pentecostal leadership. Unless the pastor or leader of the meeting is really in touch with God and able thereby to exercise true spiritual leadership, much will be lost.

There must be edification. True worship is not only glorifying to God; it is also edifying to men. It is significant that in Ephesians 5:19 Paul says that in our hymns and psalms we are "addressing one another" (RSV). Similarly, in Colossians 3:16, he points out that we are to "teach and admonish one another" through our singing. Thus, while we sing to God, we also sing to each other, and our singing should result in teaching truth and encouraging godliness.

Perhaps this is why Paul urges the Colossians to let the Word of Christ dwell in them richly, so that the hymns and spiritual songs they sing are the expression of that Word. Is not this a reminder that the words of our hymns and choruses are more important than the tunes? There is no need for us to be content with third-rate tunes, but above all we must be concerned to see that what we sing is scripturally true and expressed in a form that is both glorifying to God and edifying to ourselves. The tune may be catchy, but unless it is married to words that utter sound doctrine it has no place in the worship of the Spirit-filled Church.

There must be Spirit-inspired spontaneity. The New Testament ideal in Ephesians 5:18, 19 is of a group of believers so filled with the Spirit that their worship flows out from them in all the freshness and liveliness of a sunlit fountain, finding expression in a variety of ways. Order and meaning are vital to worship, as we have seen, but without the life and freedom of the Spirit they become a dull, repetitive routine which leaves worshipers listless and can never satisfy the heart of the living God. Paul's vision, rather, is of a group of Spirit-filled believers so responsive to the sovereign leading of the Spirit that their worship corresponds to all that He is in His essential being. Their worship is vocal ("speaking"), it is varied ("psalms and hymns and spiritual songs"), and it is vital ("singing, and making melody in your heart . . . giving thanks").

There is no set pattern for this kind of worship, yet it never becomes confused, because the Spirit of God is in control, and that control is manifested at every level—in the leader of the meeting and also in the members of the congregation. Such an atmosphere cannot be worked up or produced by human techniques; it is the direct result of the Spirit's moving in the midst.

Nothing is more disastrous than the attempt to create an "atmosphere" in a meeting. When we resort to this kind of thing, we are confessing our spiritual emptiness. Nothing is worse than the attempt to imitate the blessing of God. Painted fire never burns and plastic imitations of Pentecost never satisfy. Our retreat from the imitation, however, must not cause us to abandon our desire for the real thing. Have we lost the art of real "singing in the Spirit" because there have been times when human imitations have put us off? Have we lost something of the fervor and freedom of real Pentecost because of the misdemeanors of a few misguided enthusiasts? Perhaps we need to seek afresh for the moving of the Spirit in our midst by allowing Him greater freedom in our individual hearts.

How wonderful to be in a meeting over which the Spirit really has control, where the tidal movements of His power are felt in every heart, and where the worshipers respond to Him, now sharing with Him, perhaps, the "silence of eternity, interpreted by love," now stirring like trees in the winds as His power intensifies, now caught up in an ecstasy of praise as He makes known the glory of the Lord Jesus, voices mingling in that strange alchemy of worship which we sometimes call "singing in the Spirit," only to subside again into a reflective calm. This is the wind blowing where it listeth; this is true Spirit-born worship, and there is nothing to compare with it.

Such worship cannot be produced, but it can be prepared for. If those of us who conduct the services and those of us who attend would take more time to prepare our hearts before God and would give the Holy Spirit His rightful place in our hearts, we should know these heights of worship far more frequently than we do. George Beaseley Murray has said, "The thrill of gathering for worship consists in the fact that we are people excitedly lining the road along which at any moment Christ is going to come." Lining the route for the King—what anticipation ought to fill our hearts as we come to the house of God!

There is an ancient chest in Durham Cathedral which has five locks, and it is said that the keys to those locks were held by separate members of the Cathedral staff (evidently somebody didn't trust the treasurer!). It was impossible to get access to the contents of the chest unless the five key-bearers were present, each in possession of his particular key. Is there not a parable here? Each of us holds a key to the communal life of the assembly, and the assembly cannot gain access to its full inheritance unless we are personally present and willing to insert our individual key into its rightful place. Only as each individual member of the assembly is prepared to open his being to the Holy Spirit, and comes into the assembly with a readiness to participate fully in worship and respond to the Spirit's leading, can that assembly fully realize its identity as a worshiping community.

"Pray then," wrote Ignatius to the Ephesians, "come and join this choir, every one of you; let there be a whole symphony of minds in concert; take the tone all together from God, and sing aloud to the Father with one voice through Jesus Christ, so that He may hear you and know by your good works that you are indeed members of His Son's Body." Ancient words they may be, but words which a modern Church might well ponder.

9

Its Outreach

"Go out and blow your horn louder than ever to the glory of God." With these words a Los Angeles judge admonished "Joe the Turk," a flamboyant Salvation Army officer whose street evangelism had brought him before the court on a charge of creating a disturbance.

The judge had the good sense to realize that, with a message like the gospel to proclaim, it is impossible to keep quiet. Or is it? Certainly when the Early Church was ordered to be silent, its leaders firmly replied, "We cannot but speak the things which we have seen and heard" (Acts 4:20); but only too often their successors in our day and age seem either unwilling or unable to declare themselves.

The Church has an inescapable commitment as far as evangelism is concerned. The four Gospels bear impressive testimony to this fact. Each of them ends on this note of involvement in evangelism:

"Go ye therefore and teach all nations" (Matthew 28:19).

"Go ye into all the world, and preach the gospel to every creature" (Mark 16:15).

"And that repentance and remission of sins should be preached in his name among all nations . . . and ye are witnesses of these things" (Luke 24:47, 48).

"As my Father hath sent me, even so send I you" (John 20:21).

Neither the exciting events of those post-Resurrection days nor the truly remarkable phenomena attached to the ascension of Christ in any way lessened the impact of His words about evangelism. The Holy Spirit inspired each of the evangelists to put the emphasis of the gospel where it properly belongs. The historic facts are only completely relevant when they are declared. It is through the foolishness of preaching that the dynamics of the Cross are transmitted.

For the Spirit-filled Church this emphasis is even greater. The great promise of Acts 1:8 demonstrates this with tremendous force:

"Ye shall receive power, after that the Holy Ghost is come upon you."

"Ye shall be witnesses unto me."

With an emphatic "Ye shall" the risen Lord drives home the double truth that the promise of Pentecostal power is inseparably linked to the task of evangelism. The first "Ye shall" thrills us with the certainty of the promise; the second ought to challenge us with its unequivocal demand for action. We have no right to claim the promise unless we are prepared for the commitment.

To go back for a moment to our first chapter, if we really believe what we say we believe, we cannot but be involved in evangelism. If Jesus Christ really is the Saviour, Healer, Baptizer in the Spirit, and coming King, then the world must know it. If the gospel really is the power of God unto salvation, then it ought to be proclaimed. If the old rugged cross and the amazing triumph of the Resurrection fit together to give the combination that unlocks the gate of heaven and throws open to all men the undreamed-of resources of

God, then it ought to be published. To fail to do so is criminal.

The words of Acts 1:8 not only constitute a call to evangelism; they also provide us with a concise yet comprehensive definition of what it really is in terms of message, method, and mission.

The basic message is: "Ye shall be witnesses *unto me.*" No one can read the New Testament without being deeply impressed by the way in which, both in their preaching and writing, the apostles bore testimony to Jesus. The first recorded sermon in the Book of Acts, that of Peter on the Day of Pentecost, moved swiftly from an explanation of the Pentecostal phenomena to a detailed exposition of the person and work of Christ (Acts 2:14-36). When Philip went down to Samaria, he "preached Christ unto them" (Acts 8:5), and again in the Gaza desert, when he encountered the Ethiopian, the message was the same—he "preached unto him Jesus" (v. 35).

With this name Paul opened his ministry (Acts 9:20, 22, 29). In this name Peter first went to the Gentiles (Acts 10:36), and with this name the Book of Acts closed (Acts 28:31). One of the most striking features of the New Testament is the way in which the name of Jesus Christ dominates everything. Take, for instance, Paul's Epistle to the Philippians. In the space of 104 verses the names or titles of Jesus Christ occur at least 47 times, and beyond the mere use of His name a great deal more space is taken up with references to Him.

The Lord Jesus Christ, who He is as the divine Son of God, and what He has done as the Saviour and Redeemer of men, is the very heart of the gospel. Whatever else we may feel constrained to preach, every sermon and every act of personal testimony must be a road leading straight to Christ himself.

There is a danger that we can be so concerned with the "fringe benefits" of the gospel—things like peace of mind, happiness, divine healing, and deliverance—that we fail to lead people to that vital encounter with Christ which will result in their repentance and whole-hearted commitment to Him as Lord and Master. The advertising world knows that it can achieve a kind of conversion, especially by the "free-offer" technique. Otherwise choosy housewives can be induced to change their usual choice of cornflakes by the offer of some free article with another brand (and their professedly cynical husbands can likewise be induced to change their brand of gasoline by some similar offer). The switch is based not on a real evaluation of the product, but on the desire to get something for nothing. More often than not, the purchaser reverts to his old habits afterwards.

Is there not a lesson for us here? While it is wonderfully true that the gospel is a "free offer" of the blessing of God, which is directed to meet the many needs of men's hearts, at the same time the first task of the evangelist is to bring men and women to a confrontation with Jesus. Perhaps one reason why there are superficial "decisions" and a lack of deep conviction of sin and thoroughgoing conversion is that we have tended to focus on the benefits that accrue to us in salvation, rather than on Christ himself and His unequivocal demand for repentance and surrender.

It would be wrong to suggest that the gospel does not answer the deep needs of men. It would not be "good news" unless it had a practical bearing on the human situation. To preach Christ is not only to proclaim the mystery of His divine-human personality, but to declare that in His death and resurrection God has set forth an answer to the spiritual and moral problems of the world and opened the way to a new relationship with himself. Forgiveness, cleansing, deliverance from the power and penalty of sin, reconciliation, untold joy and inward peace are all part of the gospel, but the Cross is more than an escape hatch for trapped men. It is the doorway to the throne of Christ.

A Christian is not merely a refugee; he is a subject of Jesus Christ. Being a Christian consists not of simply changing to another brand of moral painkiller, but of submitting to a divine takeover. "If you confess ... that Jesus is Lord ... you will be saved" (Romans 10:9, RSV).

The basic method is "Ye shall be witnesses." The techniques of evangelism are so many and so varied that they would require a whole book—probably a whole library—to do them justice, but the basic method is simple. It is witnessing, that is, declaring, and affirming to be true, things which are known to us through personal experience. A witness does not merely give his opinion, or simply pass on secondhand information; he can declare with the Lord Jesus himself: "We speak that we do know, and testify that we have seen" (John 3:11), and with the apostle John: "That ... which we have heard, which we have seen with our eyes, which we have looked upon, and our hands have handled ... declare we unto you" (1 John 1:1-3). No man can be an evangelist who has not had a personal encounter with Jesus Christ.

The important point in all this is that true evangelism does not take place until the actual message of the gospel has been verbally communicated. Now there are many Christians who say, "Well, I am no good at speaking to people, but, so long as I live my life as a Christian should, I am witnessing." Is this really so? It is vital that we *live* consistent Christian lives—and how often has the testimony been ruined because of the unworthy conduct of those who professed to be followers of Christ—but the truth is that, unless the actual terms of the gospel are spelled out in simple language, evangelism cannot take place.

Our lives may corroborate the truth of the gospel, but they are no substitute for the actual message of the gospel. Unless men know *why* we live as we do—unless, that is, they are actually told the truth about the Lord Jesus and His saving power—their admiration for our way of life will never save them. "We *speak* that we do know" is the essence of evangelism.

What we have already said about commitment to Christ underlines the necessity for this. The Church is commissioned to make disciples, not to draw a crowd of admirers, and a disciple is a man who is ready to accept the discipline that Christ imposes, one who will sit as a learner at His feet, one who will walk as a follower in His steps. Our task is to persuade men (2 Corinthians 5:11), to call them to obedience to the faith (Romans 1:5), and this involves an inevitable verbal encounter. Whether it be through the more formal avenues of preaching, or through personal conversation, tract distribution, Sunday school teaching, letter writing, broadcasting, or any other form, evangelism involves the declaration of the facts about Jesus Christ, His person and work, and the offer of the grace of God in Him.

The Church should concern itself with the many human needs that call for its help, and the individual believer should be at pains to see that his behavior is consistent with his beliefs, but we must never view these things as an alternative to actually telling the Good News. They certainly have a bearing on the gospel and they demonstrate its effectiveness, but they are not substitutes for the gospel. Men are not saved by their admiration of Christians; they are saved when they hear the Word of Truth and respond to it in repentance and faith—but "how shall they hear without a preacher?"

The extent of the mission is, "beginning at Jerusalem." In one of His parables Christ defined the field of His operations as "the world" (Matthew 13:38), and in this closing message to His followers He indicates the breadth of their mission. It is to begin at Jerusalem, but it is to embrace the world.

Evangelism must be local without becoming parochial; it must be global without becoming impersonal. The Spirit-filled Church must never become so absorbed in itself and its own existence that it loses sight of the wider needs of the world.

An assembly can turn in upon itself and be engrossed in its own activities to the extent that it is insensitive to the needs of missionary endeavor in other lands and fails to play its part in the world mission of the Church. On the other hand, interest in foreign missions can become a substitute for personal evangelism. Giving to the missionary cause, some people feel, lets them out of the obligations of more personal involvement. Like long-range artillery, they send salvos of money and prayer on to distant battlefields but retreat from the hand-to-hand combat that is raging on their own doorstep. Others will travel miles to take part in an evangelistic effort of some kind or other, or will give enthusiastic support to some special outreach among drug addicts or the like on the other side of the city, but they hesitate when it comes to personal witness or taking part in the outreach of their own church. "These ought ye to have done, and not to leave the other undone."

There is no such thing as evangelism by proxy. We cannot pray or pay for others to do our witnessing for us. By all means let us give our support to the worldwide missionary cause and have a broad vision of evangelism, but let us never forget that this does not absolve us from the responsibility of witnessing to those among whom we live and work.

Nor must we overlook the importance of motive in evangelism. One of the most shocking passages in the New Testament is surely Philippians 1:15-18. Paul says that men are actually "preaching Christ" out of spite in order to outstrip the imprisoned apostle. Can it be possible? Sadly, it is. Whether in preaching, or in Sunday school or youth work, or in evangelism, it is possible to be moved by a competitive spirit, or the desire to achieve success for success's sake. We all know the temptation, and we all need to pray to be delivered from it.

The urge to evangelize can sometimes spring from a well-intentioned but misguided desire merely to recoup the losses we sustain through deaths and removals from our local churches, or our anxiety to preserve our denominational existence. Evangelism—and for that matter, any form of Christian activity—can become the offering we make at the golden calf of "Success," or a frenzied dance around the altar of Self-preservation. For one thing we may be grateful: if Christ is preached then God graciously honors His Word, even though the motives of those who evangelize may be mixed and their lives unworthy. I suppose that if we waited until we were sure our motives were free from any alloy of self-seeking we would never evangelize, but on the other hand we ought not to be content with anything that is unworthy of Jesus Christ. We need constantly to bring our hearts and our work before Him for "we persuade men; but what we are is known to God" (2 Corinthians 5:11, RSV).

The true motive for evangelism is written into the heart of the gospel: "God so loved . . . that he gave"

(John 3:16). May God help us to feel the same motivation, to say with Paul, "The love of Christ constraineth us" (2 Corinthians 5:14). This can come about only through the activity of the Holy Spirit (Romans 5:5).

The words of William Cooke, written in the latter part of the last century in a book called *The Shekinah*, are as revelant today as when they were first penned: "Without the Spirit no signs will follow, no rocky hearts will be broken down into genuine penitential sorrow, no souls will be won to Christ. Men might as well . . . call for a vital response from the moldering skeletons of a charnel house as to preach to dead souls without the influence of the Spirit of life and power. Nothing but the vital breath of the Holy Ghost can change the dry bones which fill the wide valley of death into an army of living men."

The Spirit must direct. One reason why our evangelism is sometimes ineffective is that we have lost sight of the fact that Christ is Lord of the harvest. It is not only His power that causes the seed to germinate and the Word to bear fruit, but it is also His prerogative to say which field shall be reaped and when, and who shall reap it.

His authority, not merely in a vague overall sense, but in the direct details of the actual work of evangelism, must be the basis of all our outreach. With deep sincerity and really sacrificial endeavor we can sally forth into the wrong field at the wrong time using the wrong people and the wrong methods; and instead of coming home rejoicing, bringing our sheaves with us, we trudge home despondently to organize a commission to look into more modern methods of harvesting. Having read the latest glossy brochures, we save our hard-earned money to invest in the latest machinery only to find that it gets bogged down in our particular field—and all the time the Lord himself is saying to us, "Pray ye therefore the Lord of the harvest, that he will send forth laborers into his harvest" (Matthew 9:38). It is His harvest. It is His responsibility to direct the laborers; it is our responsibility to seek Him in prayer.

The evangelistic commission of the Church is rooted firmly in the lordship of Christ. "All power [authority] is given unto me in heaven and in earth. Go ye therefore" (Matthew 28:18, 19). This authority is mediated through the Holy Spirit (see Acts 1:2). Again it needs to be stressed that the authority of Christ is not a vague *carte blanche* given to the Church in the same way that an absentee employer might authorize someone to act on his behalf, but is the direct personal involvement of Christ himself through the Spirit. It is not a kind of spiritual rubber stamp authorizing the Church to get on with the job of spreading the gospel as it sees fit, but the immediate presence of the Lord himself in the midst, personally directing the work— "the Lord working with them and confirming the word with signs following" (Mark 16:20).

No one can read the New Testament without being keenly aware of the immediacy and directness of this divine leadership. The narrative suggests not simply the presence of an overruling hand, but the consciousness on the part of the apostles that they were being led of God. They did things because they knew God wanted them to do them. Philip's movement from Samaria to Gaza (Acts 8:26, 29, 39) is an example of this, which is repeated in the experience of Peter (Acts 10:19; see also 11:12) and Paul (Acts 13:1-4; 16:6-10; 2 Corinthians 2:12).

There is a great need for the leaders of an assembly to know the direction of the Spirit. Evangelism ought to be more than a haphazard attempt to try this or that, or merely an attempt to copy something that has worked in other places. There are fads and fashions in evangelism which are as trendy as the latest productions of the Paris dress designers. Let us not follow coyly in the parade of imitators that always troop behind the bandwagon.

On the other hand, we ought not to reject anything because it happens to be new. There is need for ministers and deacons to keep abreast of what is going on in the world of evangelism. We need to read widely and to learn all that we can from the successes—and failures—of others. When all is said and done, however, we need humbly to seek to know what God desires us to do in our own particular situation.

Evangelism ought to be on the agenda of every deacons' meeting; it ought to be part of the thinking of every department of the church—not merely as just another item, but as the vital objective around which all else must be built. We must be prepared to think, and above all, to pray over this matter until we know what God would have us do.

The Spirit must empower. For all his gifts of personality and intellect, Paul was the first to recognize that success in evangelism lay not in these things but in the power of the Spirit (1 Corinthians 2:1-5; 1 Thessalonians 1:5). Again, in Romans 15:18, 19, he outlined his understanding of what evangelism really meant: "Christ has wrought through me to win obedience from the Gentiles, by word and deed, by the power of signs and wonders, by the power of the Holy Spirit, so that . . . I have fully preached the gospel of Christ" (RSV). Thus the man who was, perhaps, the greatest evangelist the Church has ever known recognized that the secret of real effectiveness in evangelism lay not in human techniques or methods so much as in the operation of the Holy Spirit, both in the life of the evangelist and in the hearts of those to whom he witnessed.

Unless there is this dual work of the Spirit, true evangelism cannot take place. Unless the evangelist speaks under the anointing of the Spirit, his words will simply be the "enticing words of man's wisdom," eloquent in form and relevant in content, but devoid of real spiritual authority. Unless the Spirit is at work in the hearts of the hearers, convicting them of "sin, and of righteousness, and of judgment," the word preached will fall on deaf ears. Unless Spirit-anointed lips speak to Spirit-convicted hearts no true communication of the gospel can take place.

Douglas Webster, in his excellent book *What is Evangelism?* has touched on this problem: "It is imperative to recognize that the Holy Ghost is the ultimate answer to the problem of communication. He is *the* Communicator." In another vivid paragraph he writes: "Communication requires a relationship of man to man or preacher to hearers, and in the sphere of human relationships and the mystery of another's mind and soul only the Holy Ghost is Lord, knowing His way around and able to achieve communication." Only the man who is prepared to give himself to prayer and the ministry of the Word so that he may learn the phraseology of the Spirit (1 Corinthians 2:13) and who recognizes that, apart from the operation of the Spirit in the hearts of his hearers, he is helpless, will ever achieve a genuine communication of the gospel. As Webster has said, only the Holy Ghost knows His way around the labyrinth of another man's soul, and unless we are humble enough to follow His leading we are likely to get hopelessly lost.

One of the forgotten factors in evangelism is the reality of the demonic. Not only in temptation do we "wrestle against principalities and powers," but also in evangelism. Paul highlights this when he declares that his commission from Christ was not only to turn men from darkness to light, but also "from the power of Satan unto God" (Acts 26:18). Whenever a man is genuinely converted it means that the satanic stranglehold has been broken. Evangelism, therefore, is not simply an attempt to persuade men to change their minds or even to "receive Christ," but a headlong encounter with the powers of darkness in which only the dynamic of the Spirit can overpower the demonic. Until we realize this awe-inspiring fact we shall never really take our preaching or witnessing as seriously as we should.

Is it not significant that at least four of the gifts of the Spirit are related in some degree to the work of evangelism? Faith, working of miracles, gifts of healings, and discerning of spirits, all have a bearing on this.

Some have exaggerated the importance of what is sometimes called "deliverance ministry," until they and their followers seem obsessed with miracles for miracles' sake. Some, in their zeal for the miraculous, have made claims not capable of authentication. We must never forget that Christ himself more than once stressed that of themselves miracles have only a limited value (Luke 16:31; John 4:48). He regarded them only as a second line of evidence, preferring men to believe His word on its own merit (John 14:11). But also we must not forget that He was a man "attested . . . by God with mighty works and wonders and signs" (Acts 2:22, RSV). Both the Gospels and the Book of Acts bear eloquent testimony that the evangelism of Christ and the apostles was greatly assisted by the miraculous.

Perhaps it is the responsibility that these gifts place upon us that causes us to hesitate. Certainly they can only be truly exercised by those who are prepared to walk in humble dependence upon and close communion with God, and in our self-confident and hectic way of life these are not popular virtues. May God help us to see our need of all that He has provided, and give us the grace to seek humbly for His full provision—and the added grace of recognizing those to whom His gifts have been given, even though in our view they are not the right people!

Evangelism calls for the total involvement of the whole assembly. That God has given evangelists to the Church is abundantly clear (Ephesians 4:11). The ministry of such gifted brethren must be recognized and utilized to the full. We might ask ourselves whether our idea of an evangelist is wide enough. Do we think of him only as the full-time man who holds crusades? Is it not possible that in our local churches there are men with evangelistic gifts who have not been called to full-time ministry? Ought we not to pray that God will help us to recognize and use the talent that may be lying dormant in our churches.

Certainly the pastor himself must "do the work of an evangelist" (2 Timothy 4:5), and he has no right to opt out of this difficult work by feeling that his gifts lie in a different direction. Through personal witness and public preaching he must be an evangelist, and he must also seek to discover and employ the gifts that are distributed in the assembly, and see that every member of the church is engaged in this supreme task.

Acts 8:1-4 makes it clear that, not only the apostles, but the rank and file of the Early Church were involved in spreading the gospel. In Philippians 1:5 Paul thanks his readers for their "fellowship in the gospel," a fellowship which involved them in earnest prayer (v. 19), dedicated living (v. 27), and active involvement in "striving together for the faith of the gospel" (v. 27). In Philippians 4:14 he thanks them for the financial support they have given in the cause of evangelism. Again, in 1 Thessalonians 1:8 he congratulates the assembly on the fact that it has become a sounding board for the gospel, and the word he uses implies a *continuous* sound. The Church at Thessalonica was involved in continuous evangelism, by means of which the gospel was being disseminated throughout the whole area.

Our churches must become bases where Christians are trained in evangelism, where prayer is centered on the needs of men, and where those who are brought in will hear the gospel effectively preached. Our homes must become mission stations. Our personal lives must become "mobile units" by which the Spirit of God can touch the lives of those whom we meet day by day in the normal encounters of life.

The Spirit-filled church really has no option but to evangelize.

10

Its Continuance

Every spiritual movement faces the danger of eventual decline. One of the most solemn features of the New Testament is that the opening chapters of its final Book have to deal with the decline of the first Pentecostal churches in Asia Minor.

Ephesus had been born in the fires of Pentecostal fervor and had flourished under the ministry of men like Paul and John, but in the passage of years it lost its first love; and Sardis, for all its reputation of being a live church, had become spiritually dead. The bank account at Laodicea was impressive, but spiritually the Church was bankrupt. This is the constant peril that every church must face. No church, however illustrious its beginnings, is immune to the possibility of decline; therefore no church can ever afford to relax its watchfulness or neglect the true sources of its ongoing life.

We can lose our Spirit-filled condition because of what J. H. Jowett once called "a deadening familiarity with the sublime." We can become so used to Pentecostal blessing that we cease really to value it; it becomes commonplace.

To quote Jowett again: "A man may live in mountain country and lose all sense of the heights." Think for a moment of the tremendous implications of Pentecostal worship: a congregation under the direct control of the Third Person of the Trinity and responding to His direction like an orchestra obeying its conductor. What possibilities are present in such a situation!

Think of the implications of the genuine exercise of the gifts of the Spirit: God himself breaking in to express himself in an amazingly contemporaneous way within the family circle of His gathered people. Yet these astounding things can become just parts of the routine to which we have become accustomed. When this happens we are on the way to losing our heritage.

To lose our sense of wonder is to lose our sense of values, and when we no longer value the gifts of God we are in danger of letting them slip through our fingers. When the burning bush becomes just another bush, the desert is beginning to close in again.

We can lose our Spirit-filled condition because of an inhibiting fear of the supernatural. This takes many forms, but basically it has a close relationship to what we have already said. When Christians fail to appreciate the truly wonderful nature of genuine Pentecostal experience and lose their sense of holy awe, they inevitably cheapen the whole thing. After a while it becomes relatively easy to say, "Thus saith the Lord," and once that happens Pentecostal standards are devalued and soon cheap human imitations begin to appear. As a result, sincere men and women are turned aside. They find it difficult to distinguish between what may be genuine and what is "of the flesh." In the end, they lose their respect for anything that is "Pentecostal," even though they remain in the fellowship of a Pentecostal assembly. In the same way, pastors, through fear of unfortunate incidents, opt for the easy way out by discouraging, or at least not encouraging, the exercise of spiritual gifts in the assembly.

These attitudes are understandable—but they are

deadly to the continuance of a Spirit-filled condition. Ultimately they lead to the cynicism which takes everything with a pinch of salt, and cynicism is the osteoarthritis of a Pentecostal church. It is crippling.

We can lose our Spirit-filled condition by substituting the natural for the spiritual. Once the retreat from the supernatural gets under way, natural alternatives become essential. This is the point of Paul's question to the Galatians: "Having begun in the Spirit, are you now ending with the flesh?" By inference the situation is absurd. Can that which is essentially spiritual find its ultimate fulfillment in forms which are merely natural?

Can you reproduce the full crimson glory of a sunset on a sepia postcard? This is what you are reduced to when you abandon the true glory of Pentecostal life and worship. The substitutes are elaborate: complex structures of church organization, impressive ceremonies, magnificent buildings, gorgeous music, eloquent preaching, financial security, modern techniques, and smooth-tongued psychology. These can no more take the place of a real Spirit-filled condition than plastic flowers can take the place of daisies in the springtime woodland. Many of these things may be necessary, at least to some degree, but they are not an alternative for the ongoing life of the Spirit.

"Liberty," said Bernard Shaw, "means responsibility. That's why most men dread it." The cost of Pentecostal liberty in terms of responsibility is a high one, and that is why many pastors and churches seek alternatives. That there are problems in Pentecostal practice is undeniable—but all genuine life brings problems. Every mother and father knows this. The leadership of a Pentecostal church places great responsibilities upon the pastor. He must learn to recognize the leading of the Spirit and to discern between what is of the Spirit and what is of the flesh. He may sometimes have the difficult task of dealing with those who are out of order—even at the cost of being misunderstood—but this is the price that he must be willing to pay for the privilege of maintaining a well-ordered but lively assembly. The price is definitely worth it. Better to have Pentecostal life and liberty, with all its problems, than the orderly peace of a cemetery.

So it is also for the members of the church. The enemy of Pentecost is spiritual lethargy—the willingness to accept a second- or third-rate level of spiritual experience because the disciplines of a true Pentecostal condition are too demanding. Some people are prepared to accept Pentecostal doctrine without seeking a Pentecostal experience. Others enjoy the blessing of a Pentecostal atmosphere without ever contributing to it. They live off the spiritual capital provided by other people. Others retreat from Pentecostal practice because they resent any attempt by the pastor to correct their mistakes, and refuse to listen to any other than their own opinions.

The reasons for Pentecostal decline are numerous, but none of them is valid. When all is said and done, it is possible for any Christian and any church to enjoy the full spiritual heritage which the risen Christ bestowed upon His Church on the Day of Pentecost, and it is possible for that man and that church through humble, obedient dependence on the Holy Spirit to maintain a high order of spiritual life, come what may.

"Pentecost," said James S. Stewart, "did not happen in a vacuum. It happened in an atmosphere where faith and eagerness had prepared the way. It came to men who were taking time to listen for God. . . . It is the listless, bored, apathetic, nonexpectant attitude that baulks God all along the line. . . . It is the expectant heart to which the Holy Spirit comes" (*The Gates of New Life*). How true this is, not only of the first out-pouring of the Spirit, but also of the continuance of a Pentecostal condition.

We must never forget that we are utterly dependent upon the Spirit. We may have an educated ministry and a beautiful church building. We may have excellent resources in terms of money and facilities. We may have talented and enthusiastic members and all the natural advantages one can think of. Without the presence and power of the Holy Spirit, however, we are helpless. This should drive us continually to seek for the continuing work of the Spirit in our midst. "They continued steadfastly" is the description the Spirit approvingly records in Acts 2:42. Unless this is recorded of us another, more sinister, word will be written over us—"Ichabod," the glory has departed.

Pentecostal churches require Pentecostal leadership. Unless the pastor maintains his Pentecostal convictions and his own Pentecostal experience, the church will suffer. "Like pastor, like people" is a true maxim. The pastor must give himself to prayer and the ministry of the Word (Acts 6:4). He must, like Timothy, be ready to "stir up the gift" that has been given to him. The future of the Pentecostal Movement lies not in its conferences, its denominational structures, or its ambitious programs for expansion, but in the simple spirituality of its pastors and local leaders.

This is why we must give attention to the training of men for the ministry, not only to equip them academically, but also to prepare them spiritually. To a great extent the future lies in what is happening in the Bible colleges, for it is there that future leadership is being molded. We need to pray earnestly for all who are engaged in this vital work, and we need, too, continually to uphold all those who by virtue of their

110

pastoral calling hold the key to so much. "Brethren, pray for us."

The deacons and church officers have a tremendous responsibility too. Unless the deacons are men of strong Pentecostal convictions and *contemporary* Pentecostal experience, the local church will suffer. Unless the Sunday school staff, youth workers, and other leaders are Spirit-filled, the church will likewise suffer. I have said "contemporary experience" in this context because it is not enough for a man to have had a past experience of Pentecostal blessing. Better a man who has not received the baptism in the Spirit, but who is thirsting for more of God, than the man who had an experience 20 years ago and has forgotten all about it. It is neither desirable nor practicable to make the baptism in the Spirit the only criterion by which a man's eligibility for office is judged, though Acts 6:3 reminds us that the apostles did insist on Spirit-filled men even for the administration of the widows' fund; but if a church is to maintain its Pentecostal character for very long it must be led by those who are prepared continually to seek to be filled and to remain filled with the Spirit.

A Pentecostal church consists not only of Pentecostal leaders but Pentecostal people, people who are willing to obey the call of the New Testament to be continually filled with the Spirit. This means that every member of the church must seek to maintain his personal walk with God, to guard against the things that would diminish his spiritual life, and to pour into the assembly the resources he has derived through his personal encounter with the Spirit.

The Spirit-filled church must be prepared for change. The continuity of Pentecostal blessing does not necessarily mean conformity to tradition. Every now and then God does a "new thing." Every now and

111

then the Spirit breaks across accepted patterns and initiates a new development of His purpose. The new wine is continually bursting old bottles, and it is well to remember that so far as church structures or the format of meetings go, today's new bottles may become tomorrow's old ones. We must be prepared, like Peter at Joppa (Acts 10:19), to "think on the vision" and if necessary to abandon our traditions and prejudices in order to keep in step with the Spirit. The central truths of Pentecost are unchanging, but the outward forms in which they are expressed may change. The truly Spirit-filled church is the one which is sensitive to the leading of the Spirit and able to adapt its ways to His.

We are living on the outer fringe of history, before that "great and notable day of the Lord come." We may well be the last columns of the Church Militant to march across the arena of time. God grant that the Church of the last days shall be like the Church of the first days—a glorious company of men and women, saved by the blood of Christ, filled with the Spirit of God, manifesting the gifts of the Spirit, adorned by the fruit of the Spirit, witnessing and ministering in the power of the Spirit, and worshiping the risen Lord under the anointing of the Spirit—in short, *a Spirit-filled Church.*